CRYPTOCURRENCY SECRETS

FOR BEGINNERS

LUCAS STERLING

TOP TIER PRESS

Published under the author brand **Lucas Sterling**

This edition contains material originally published separately as:

Book One: ***Cryptocurrency for Complete Beginners*** **© 2025 Top Tier Press**

Book Two: ***Cryptocurrency Investing 101*** **© 2025 Top Tier Press**

CONTENTS

PART ONE
CRYPTOCURRENCY FOR COMPLETE BEGINNERS

CONTENTS

PART ONE
CRYPTOCURRENCY FOR COMPLETE BEGINNERS

PART TWO
CRYPTOCURRENCY INVESTING 101

PART ONE

CRYPTOCURRENCY FOR COMPLETE BEGINNERS

THE ULTIMATE INVESTOR'S GUIDE TO BITCOIN, ETHEREUM, ALTCOINS, NFTS, AND BLOCKCHAIN - LEARN TO INVEST SMART, MANAGE RISK, AND RIDE THE NEXT MILLIONAIRE-MAKING WAVE

INTRODUCTION

Imagine you're standing at the edge of a vast, mysterious landscape. In the distance, you hear about fortunes being made, new tools for creative freedom, and even money that moves at the speed of thought. The word "crypto" echoes everywhere from your friends' WhatsApp chats to headlines on your social media feeds to late-night conversations with colleagues who say, "I just bought some Bitcoin." On one hand, it sounds thrilling, a whole new world of possibility. On the other hand, all the noise and jargon make it feel risky, complicated, and maybe even a little bit scary.

You might be wondering: Is cryptocurrency really worth my attention? Isn't this just another overhyped trend people will laugh about in five years? Am I too late, or worse, already left behind?

Let's be clear from the outset: cryptocurrency is more than just hype. It's a revolution quietly reshaping how people around the world think about and use money. For decades, we've relied on banks and middlemen to move value across borders, to store our savings, or to power new businesses. However, cryptocurrency has managed to unlock those previously unattainable opportunities. Suddenly, anyone with a smartphone and an internet connection, no matter where they live, can participate in this new financial universe.

Why is this such a big deal? For the first time in modern history, ordinary people, not governments or mega-corporations, are rewriting the rules of money. You don't need a PhD, a Wall Street job, or even prior experience investing. Crypto puts powerful financial tools in your hands, inviting you to join a global experiment in innovation, ownership, and opportunity.

But let's be honest: if you're reading this, there's a good chance you're feeling overwhelmed. Every search for "crypto investing" seems to reveal a plethora of technical terms, including blockchains, wallets, miners, forks, NFTs, DeFi, and more. One blog says you're missing out if you don't buy today. Another warns it's all a giant bubble. And every guide feels written for either rocket scientists or reckless gamblers, not careful, curious beginners like you.

That's why this book exists: to cut through the chaos, demystify the basics, and give you a solid foundation, regardless of your background. You don't need to know anything about programming, finance, economics, or cryptography. If you can use a smartphone and shop online, you have everything it takes to understand and benefit from the crypto movement.

So, what will you gain from these pages? Three things: understanding, action, and confidence.

First, you'll learn the "why" behind cryptocurrency, not just what it does, but why it matters. We'll start with simple stories and real-world examples: sending money overseas without sky-high fees, protecting your savings from inflation, or artists selling digital masterpieces directly to fans without big tech platforms taking a cut. You'll see how blockchain technology works without getting lost in complicated algorithms or code.

Second, we'll focus on practical steps. This isn't theory; it's your beginner's handbook. You'll discover how to safely set up your first digital wallet, choose and buy your first coins, keep your investments secure, and dodge the most common scams and mistakes. No step will be skipped. Each explanation is broken down into plain English, as if I were walking you through it, side by side.

And finally, you'll walk away with confidence. Crypto can be volatile and confusing, but it doesn't have to be intimidating. Knowledge is your shield against hype, fear, and impulsive decisions. By the end of this book, you'll know which risks to watch out for, how to spot red flags, and how to grow your position slowly and smartly. You'll be able to join the conversation about digital assets not just with curiosity, but with clarity and poise.

Now, if you've ever felt like learning about crypto is like cracking some secret code, let me reassure you: jargon stops here. You won't find any unnecessary acronyms, heart-pounding price charts, or endless rabbit holes of tech-speak. Everything you need to get started is explained in down-to-earth language, using everyday analogies and plenty of real-life scenarios. When terms come up, and sometimes they must, I'll break them down on the spot, so nothing slips by unnoticed or unexplained.

Who is this book for? For anyone who's ever watched from the sidelines, wishing they could ask "dumb questions" without judgment. For the careful, cautious investor who wants to build wealth and security, not chase quick thrills. For young professionals looking to diversify their portfolios beyond traditional stocks and bonds. For freelancers, artists, and entrepreneurs curious about new ways to create and get paid. For anyone tired of feeling locked out of important financial conversations simply because they don't speak the lingo.

If you've already tried searching for answers online, you know how easy it is to drown in conflicting advice. One influencer screams, "BUY NOW!" while another swears everything is doomed. Reddit threads spiral into memes and inside jokes. You're left more confused than when you started. Here, you'll find an island of calm: straightforward guidance, real facts, and actionable steps, nothing more, nothing less.

Let me also make a promise: it's okay to be skeptical. You should ask tough questions. Not everything about crypto is golden, and yes, there are risks. There have been scams, wild price swings, and exaggerated promises. This book will show you both the bright opportunities and the pitfalls, the exciting innovations and the traps to avoid. With the right knowledge, you'll steer clear of costly mistakes and hype-driven panic.

So, whether you want to buy your first Bitcoin, learn what Ethereum actually does, explore NFTs and digital art, or simply understand what all your friends are talking about, you're in the right place. Together, we'll tackle everything step by step, building your confidence and turning the unknown into something familiar and even empowering.

You don't have to leap headfirst into the wild world of crypto. You just have to take the first step, armed with the right information and a sense of curiosity. My goal is to turn your caution into clarity and your intrigue into action. Let's pull back the curtain, cast aside the jargon, and see what the future of money really looks like.

Ready? Your journey into the world of cryptocurrency starts here, and it's for everyone, especially you.

UNLOCK YOUR CRYPTO MASTERY TOOLKIT

Ready to take control of your digital wealth with clarity and confidence?

As a thank-you for reading this book, I've created a practical guide: **The Crypto Mastery Toolkit.** This hands-on guide simplifies key crypto concepts, helps you secure your assets, and builds confidence as you manage your digital wealth. It's designed to help you learn and apply crypto knowledge with ease and clarity.

What's included in this resource:

- Understand key crypto concepts and terminology
- Learn strategies for secure asset management
- Discover best practices for wallets, exchanges, and safety
- Develop confidence navigating today's digital economy

👉 **Access Your Companion Workbook**
Visit: **https://content.toptierpress.com/unlock-free-crypto-mastery-toolkit**

Or scan the QR code below to get instant access!

CHAPTER 1
WHAT IS CRYPTOCURRENCY, REALLY?

Well over 2 billion people worldwide still lack access to traditional banking services, yet many of them carry smartphones capable of connecting to the internet. Imagine sending money across borders without waiting days or paying high fees, or owning a form of currency that isn't controlled by any government or bank. This is no longer just a possibility; it's happening every day through cryptocurrency. But what exactly is this digital money, and how does it work when there's nothing physical to hold or a bank teller to visit? The basic differences between cryptocurrency and the cash we use daily can feel confusing at first, especially if you're new to finance or technology. Yet beneath the surface lies a system built on transparency, security, and freedom that challenges the way we think about money. This chapter takes you inside the basics of cryptocurrency and blockchain technology, offering clear insights into why these innovations matter today and why millions are beginning to see crypto as more than just headlines or hype.

Understanding Cryptocurrency: How It Differs from Regular Money and How Blockchain Works

Money has always meant something you can hold in your hand or see in your bank account. Dollars, euros, and yen are familiar because they come as coins, bills, or numbers controlled by banks or governments. Cryptocurrency flips this idea. There is no stack of crypto coins in anyone's pocket. Everything happens online, using computer codes. Bitcoin, Ethereum, and other cryptocurrencies exist because people agree to recognize streams of numbers and letters as valuable, not because some treasury created them or a bank approves each transaction.

The control of traditional money sits with governments and central banks. When the government prints dollars or the European Central Bank manages euros, they can influence how much is in use. Cryptocurrency, on the other hand, isn't managed by any country or company. The rules are built right into the software itself. Anyone with access to the internet can use crypto. There is no branch manager, bank teller, or official anywhere who decides who gets to join or what they can do. Instead, computer networks run by regular people all over the globe take care of everything through code.

The supply is another big difference. Central banks can choose to create new money whenever they believe it's needed, which sometimes leads to inflation. With Bitcoin, the maximum amount that will ever exist is set from the very beginning. There will never be more than 21 million Bitcoins. The software controls this, and nobody can change it. Some other cryptocurrencies set their limits in different ways, but the core idea is that the rules about new money creation are transparent and can't be quietly altered.

Crypto is also borderless. Picture trying to send money from one country to another. With regular money, you might need to deal with transfer fees, exchange rates, and waiting days for everything to clear. Cryptocurrency can be sent anywhere, to anyone, day or

night, with just a digital address and an internet connection. There are no weekends or bank holidays in this world.

All cryptocurrencies depend on blockchain technology. To grasp how a blockchain works, think of a ledger, like the kind old shopkeepers used, but imagine it's not stored in one dusty back room. Instead, thousands of people have the exact same copy on their computers. Every time someone sends or receives cryptocurrency, the transaction is written in the ledger. New transactions are gathered together in groups called "blocks." A block might contain dozens or hundreds of transactions.

Once a block is full, it's locked and added to the chain of blocks; that's where the name "blockchain" comes from. Every computer with a copy of the ledger checks over this new block to make sure everything adds up and that nobody is trying to fake a record. This checking process is public and open. If someone tries to lie, like claiming to have more Bitcoin than they do, the other computers will ignore it because it doesn't match their records. This setup makes cheating almost impossible.

Imagine this: Bob wants to send Alice some Bitcoin. He opens his crypto app, types in Alice's digital address, and enters the amount. His app puts the details together and sends them out to the network. Each computer on the network checks, "Does Bob really have enough Bitcoin?" If the answer is yes, Bob's balance goes down, and Alice's position goes up in the shared ledger. A record of the payment joins a group of other transactions inside a block. Soon, that block is added forever to the blockchain, where anyone in the world can see it.

People use cryptocurrencies for more than sending money. Some buy their morning coffee using crypto by scanning a code at checkout if the café accepts it. Others use cryptocurrency apps to send money home to family in another country. These transfers arrive in minutes, and the fees are often far lower than with regular banks or Western Union. Many see crypto as a way to invest, hoping the price of Bitcoin or Ethereum will rise so they can sell later at a profit. Digital art, collectibles, and even tickets to events are now bought and sold using crypto.

Trust in cryptocurrency comes from how open the system is. The rules are set in public software that anyone can search and inspect. All transactions are visible on the blockchain for everyone to check, so there are no hidden changes or back room deals. The security of the network comes from thousands of computers cross-checking every transaction, making it far harder for anyone to cheat or control the system alone.

Learning what sets cryptocurrency apart from regular cash opens the door to bigger questions. Crypto isn't just a new way to pay for things or a digital coin to invest in. Its open, shared, world-spanning design offers a new vision for how people move value and make agreements. More ideas about openness, choice, and even the freedom to run your own financial life start to come into view, inviting you to see what else might be possible.

The Importance and Impact of Crypto: Decentralization, Transparency, Freedom, and Real-World Applications

Cryptocurrency stands out because it offers something people have rarely had before: true control over their money in a digital world. With traditional banks, a few powerful players decide the rules. They can block or delay transactions, add fees, limit access during crises, or freeze accounts. Cryptocurrency reverses this through decentralization, a big word for a simple idea. No single person, company, or government acts as the boss. Instead, many computers worldwide run the network, each sharing the job and checking on the others.

Imagine sending money to a family member overseas. With banks, the money passes through several stops, each adding costs and delays. Cryptocurrency, such as Bitcoin or Ethereum, allows people to send funds directly, often in minutes, with much smaller fees. There is no gatekeeper slowing things down.

Decentralization also means equal access. Older systems sometimes shut people out, such as those without the right paperwork to open a bank account or anyone trapped by unstable policies in their home country. Picture a woman running a small business where banks are unreliable or corruption is common. By using cryptocurrency, she can protect her earnings, pay suppliers in other countries, and join a global market. Her story looks different because she no longer relies on a single company or government to control her financial future.

This network structure also makes cryptocurrency fairer. No single actor can decide who gets to use the system or change the rules behind closed doors. For people in countries facing runaway inflation or strict financial controls, this can mean holding money that keeps its value instead of watching savings disappear overnight. It offers a real chance to bypass middlemen, placing more hope and resources in the hands of ordinary people.

Transparency works differently in cryptocurrency than in banks or most companies. Each transaction lives on the blockchain, a public digital record that anyone can inspect. Although wallets use anonymous addresses instead of names, the movement of money is visible to everyone. This makes fraud or double spending much harder to carry out unnoticed. For example, a charity can share its donation address, allowing anyone to see when funds arrive and how they are spent. Donors can follow their money's journey step by step, which builds trust.

Ethical supply chains also benefit from this transparency. Imagine buying a bag of coffee. Retailers could include a code that lets customers trace the beans' entire path from farm to factory to store shelf directly on the blockchain. This helps shoppers avoid products linked to unfair labor or environmental harm and shifts power toward honest producers and informed consumers.

Financial freedom is much more than a catchphrase when traditional financial systems exclude or restrict millions. Consider a refugee resettling in a new country, unable to open a bank account due to missing paperwork. With a simple smartphone, they can create a digital wallet, store savings in cryptocurrency, and join economic life faster than any paperwork would allow. For many, cryptocurrency becomes a tool for basic dignity, not just investment.

Beyond these core ideas, the practical uses of cryptocurrency and blockchain reach into many parts of everyday life. Sending remittances, or money sent home by workers abroad, often involves high fees, long waits, and heavy paperwork. Crypto tools make this process faster and cheaper, allowing instant low-cost transfers almost anywhere in the world. Services like Litecoin or Stellar can move money in seconds, often for just a few cents per transaction. For families living far apart, this kind of access can be a lifeline.

Many people around the world still lack traditional banking services. They may have smartphones but no checking or savings account. Cryptocurrency offers them a way to save, pay, and borrow using only a digital wallet and an internet connection. Microloans, insurance, and other financial services can run through smart contracts, which are automatic programs on the blockchain that replace middlemen with transparent and consistent rules.

Digital creators find new ways to control and profit from their work too. Artists and musicians sell their art directly using NFTs (non-fungible tokens), proving ownership and getting paid without big corporations as middlemen. Someone who draws or makes music can sell directly to fans, who in turn can verify they own the real thing.

Decentralized finance, or DeFi, lets anyone lend, borrow, or earn interest with just a digital wallet. There's no need to ask a bank manager or face tough loan rules. You use platforms where the code handles everything, and everyone can see the rules.

The real shift lies in who gets to join and benefit from digital and financial systems. Blockchain ensures that no single player holds all the power. Openness, where anyone can see, verify, or build something new, leads to fairer systems. From tracking goods in shipping to securing elections against tampering and making global trade smoother, blockchain technology is already proving its impact across many industries. While price fluctuations often dominate the headlines, the deeper story of blockchain is about freedom, trust, and access. These ideas have the potential to transform far more than just money.

Now that we understand how cryptocurrency differs from traditional money and the role blockchain technology plays, we can see why this digital shift matters. Crypto offers a new way to control and move money without relying on banks or governments, opening doors for anyone with internet access to participate in a global financial system. Its transparency, security, and borderless nature provide tools for greater freedom, fairness, and opportunity, especially for those often left out of traditional finance. As you start your journey into buying and investing in crypto, this foundation gives you the confidence to navigate the space wisely, avoid common pitfalls, and explore the many ways digital assets might fit into your financial future.

CHAPTER 2
MEET THE STARS – BITCOIN AND ETHEREUM

"Why should I trust something that isn't printed by a bank or backed by a government?" That's a question many people ask when they first hear about Bitcoin and Ethereum. It's natural to feel cautious about digital money that exists only on the internet, especially if you're new to cryptocurrency. But behind this new form of value lies more than just virtual coins. It represents a revolution in how we think about money, ownership, and trust.

These two cryptocurrencies have captured the world's attention because they offer radically different ways to manage finance and technology without relying on traditional institutions. Understanding their unique roles is essential to making smart choices in the fast-changing world of crypto. This chapter will guide you step by step through what makes Bitcoin and Ethereum stand out, helping you understand why millions of people around the globe are beginning to rely on them.

Understanding Bitcoin and Ethereum: Their Strengths, Roles, and Market Dominance

Bitcoin began as the world's first cryptocurrency, launched in 2009. At its core, Bitcoin offers a digital form of money that isn't managed by any one government, company, or person. This structure means no central bank can print more of it or devalue what people already own. Bitcoin's code sets a maximum of 21 million coins that will ever exist. People sometimes call it "digital gold" because, just like gold, Bitcoin offers scarcity and a reliable way to hold value over time even when traditional banks struggle or currencies lose strength.

For many people in countries facing political or financial turmoil, banks may freeze assets, limit withdrawals, or prevent money transfers abroad. Bitcoin helps anyone bypass these limits. Owning Bitcoin means controlling your money directly, since only you hold the "keys" to your funds. Even if a government tried to censor transactions, the Bitcoin network's design makes it nearly impossible to block or reverse a legitimate transfer. People have sent Bitcoin across borders during times of crisis when wallets, banks, or even physical cash were unavailable. Wherever the internet reaches, Bitcoin transactions can go there too.

Security is another feature that draws people to Bitcoin. The system keeps track of all coins and transfers through a shared digital ledger called a blockchain. Thousands of computers all over the planet work together to verify every transaction, and once a transfer is recorded, it can't be changed or faked. This setup makes stealing Bitcoin or forging its history extremely difficult. At the same time, no individual or organization can interfere with the network's basic rules. All these aspects create a sense of reliability for those looking to protect their wealth against inflation or unstable economies.

While Bitcoin focuses mainly on being a secure and limited store of value, Ethereum takes the idea of digital money and expands what's possible. Imagine a vending machine: you put in money, make a selection, and the machine immediately gives out your snack if you've paid the right amount. No shopkeeper needs to stand by the machine that runs the transaction as a fixed rule. Ethereum uses a digital version of this logic called a smart contract. A smart contract is a bit of blockchain-based code that runs exactly as programmed, handling agreements and transactions automatically without the need for a third party.

Ethereum's platform lets anyone create these self-executing contracts, which power a growing ecosystem of decentralized tools and applications. These range from online games and social clubs to peer-to-peer lending and digital art markets. One of the largest changes Ethereum brought was making it easier for people to build new ideas on top of a blockchain. This has unlocked industries like NFTs, which certify ownership of digital items (such as artwork), and DeFi (Decentralized Finance), which offers banking tools without involving a bank at all. Whether it's borrowing, lending, trading, or launching a new kind of software, developers build these services thanks to Ethereum's programmable foundation.

Bitcoin and Ethereum hold the top two spots in the world of digital assets. Each plays a special role:

Bitcoin stands out because:

- It's the most widely recognized cryptocurrency in the world
- People trust its safety record and steady supply
- It's often used as a "set and forget" store of value, much like putting savings in a solid safe

Ethereum stands out because:

- Its technology enables new types of applications, not just currency
- Innovators can launch products and services directly on Ethereum's network
- Its system is more flexible, letting new features and projects grow rapidly

Bitcoin often leads the market because of its history, stability, and simple goal: be digital gold. Investors see it as a reliable starting point, and it tends to drive public confidence in cryptocurrency. Ethereum, by contrast, is seen as the playground for builders and creators. That's why most of today's action, products, and trends in crypto come from the world of Ethereum.

Both coins lead the market by total value held and traded by people worldwide. This dominance makes them the first choice for new users, while most businesses offering crypto payments support these two before others. The large communities and vast amount of information around Bitcoin and Ethereum help protect beginners from the risks that come with lesser-known currencies.

Getting to know the basic features and strengths of Bitcoin and Ethereum is a wise entry point for anyone exploring cryptocurrency. Their success has encouraged a wave of trust and mainstream interest, giving newcomers a safer path, solid information, and less risk of falling into scams. By focusing on their main purposes, digital gold for saving, and a smart, flexible platform for building beginners can make decisions with more clarity.

Bitcoin and Ethereum might lead together, but what sets them apart in everyday use and which fits different needs best? The next step is examining their practical differences and how each shines in real-world situations.

Key Differences Between Bitcoin and Ethereum with Real-World Use Cases

Bitcoin and Ethereum may seem alike at first because both use blockchains and allow people to send value digitally, but their technologies work in distinct ways that shape how they are used in everyday life. Bitcoin's system centers around one core goal: to record transactions in a way that is secure, trustworthy, and almost impossible to change. Every block in Bitcoin's blockchain is a simple record of transactions such as "Alice sent 1 BTC to Bob" or "Carol received 0.5 BTC from Dave." The entire network is built around a single question: can everyone trust that these records are accurate and permanent? By focusing only on transactions, Bitcoin keeps things simple and solid, earning its reputation as "battle-tested."

Ethereum was built from the start to do much more. Its blockchain doesn't just track who sent what to whom. It also contains small programs called smart contracts. These contracts are pieces of code that sit inside Ethereum's blocks and carry out instructions automatically. Unlike Bitcoin, Ethereum's system is like a digital computer that anyone can use to build applications. When someone writes a smart contract, they essentially upload a robot employee who works on the blockchain, following orders without mistakes or taking sides. This makes Ethereum flexible. People can invent new kinds of agreements, build online games, make digital art, or even create entire banking systems, none of which could work on Bitcoin.

Comparing Use Cases

The result is a split in what each platform is best known for. Bitcoin is considered a store of value, the digital version of gold. Its main purpose is to keep value safe and let it move across borders without asking anyone's permission. People use it to save money, send it to family across the world, or protect their savings in places where banks aren't safe. Companies and even a few countries keep part of their financial reserves in Bitcoin because its supply is limited. You can imagine someone in Argentina wanting to save in something safer than the local currency; putting their savings into Bitcoin can help shield them if their money loses value quickly. Or think about a family member in the United States sending Bitcoin home to relatives; they might skip the slow, expensive bank process, and the fees disappear.

Ethereum, on the other hand, is more like a playground for new ideas in finance, art, and business. It's used to build programs that can create, trade, or manage digital goods. Ethereum powers platforms where you can lend money, earn interest, swap tokens, or trade digital collectibles called NFTs (non-fungible tokens). For instance, an artist draws a digital painting, creates an NFT of it on Ethereum, and sells that NFT through a global marketplace. The buyer then owns the official, unique version of the digital art. Or a programmer might code a lending app where users can borrow and lend money out, fully automated by smart contracts, never needing a bank in the middle.

Real-World Scenarios

To see the difference in action, imagine two friends: Maya and Lucas. Maya lives in Canada but wants to send money to her parents in the Philippines every month. She buys Bitcoin, sends it straight to her family, and they exchange it for local money. The transaction takes moments, costs very little, and avoids bank delays.

Lucas is a graphic designer who creates digital posters and wants to sell them globally. He uses Ethereum to mint NFTs for his artwork. Through an NFT marketplace, collectors buy these pieces, and the smart contract ensures Lucas gets paid right away. Lucas never had to open a shop or worry about international payment systems; Ethereum handled it all.

Key Industries Using Bitcoin and Ethereum

A few industries rely on Bitcoin and Ethereum in strikingly different ways:

Finance

- **With Bitcoin:** People and businesses use it for fast, secure international payments or as a hedge against unstable national currencies.
- **With Ethereum:** The world of decentralized finance (DeFi) lives here. Borrowing, lending, trading, all happen automatically through smart contracts, with no middleman.

Art & Collectibles

- **With Ethereum:** NFTs let artists prove ownership and sell digital creations. Buyers can securely trade these assets, knowing the smart contract locks in the rules of the exchange.

Supply Chains

- **With Ethereum:** Companies write smart contracts so every step of a shipment is tracked, recorded, and visible. This brings honesty and proof into how goods move from maker to buyer, cutting the risk of fraud.

While both Bitcoin and Ethereum use blockchains to change how people move value and information, the backbone of each platform means they fit different roles. Bitcoin is steady and reliable, a place to save money or send it safely. Ethereum is for building, experimenting, and running new kinds of applications. Knowing how these differences work in everyday life helps investors and users make better choices in the world of crypto.

Now that we have explored the unique strengths and real-world uses of Bitcoin and Ethereum, newcomers can better understand how these two leading cryptocurrencies fit into today's digital economy. Bitcoin offers a secure, trusted way to save and transfer value across borders, much like digital gold, while Ethereum opens doors for creative applications, from finance to art, through its smart contract technology. With this foundation, readers are ready to make informed choices about which platform suits their personal goals and risk tolerance. By focusing on what each coin does best, anyone curious about crypto can move forward with greater confidence, avoiding common pitfalls and stepping into the world of digital assets with clarity and purpose.

CHAPTER 3

ALTCOINS EXPLAINED (AND WHICH TO WATCH)

More than 10,000 cryptocurrencies are available today, yet only a handful have lasting value and real-world use. For many newcomers, the world of altcoins and any digital currency beyond Bitcoin can feel overwhelming and confusing. Different coins promise faster payments, stronger privacy, or new ways to use money online. But behind every name and ticker symbol lies a story about who created it, what purpose it serves, and whether it's built to last or just chasing attention. Many people dive in hoping to catch a quick win but end up lost amid hype, hidden risks, and unclear goals. Understanding how to tell which altcoins are meaningful and which ones carry danger is key to making smart, confident choices as you explore the growing crypto landscape. This chapter will guide you through that process step by step.

Understanding Altcoins and Their Types

The word "altcoin" simply means any cryptocurrency that is not Bitcoin. Bitcoin came first, and its purpose was clear: a trusted electronic form of money not controlled by governments or banks. Shortly after Bitcoin's launch, developers and entrepreneurs began designing alternatives for all sorts of new uses and ideas. That's where "alt," meaning "alternative," comes from. Altcoins aren't just copycats; they are digital currencies and tokens built to solve problems, fill gaps, or experiment with new technology. Some are very different from Bitcoin, while others just tweak how it works. For anyone new to crypto, it's useful to see Bitcoin as the original and altcoins as all the new digital currencies that came after.

Altcoins exist because Bitcoin, while groundbreaking, does not do everything. After Bitcoin's rise, creators saw opportunities for coins with faster transaction speeds, greater privacy, new security options, or even ways to program rules right into their currencies. As a result, the crypto world started to grow rapidly, with each altcoin carving out its own possible use. Ethereum is a leading example. Instead of focusing only on payments, Ethereum introduced "smart contracts," self-running software programs that complete deals or handle transactions according to rules you set. These smart contracts opened the gate for new online businesses and applications. Litecoin arrived as a "lighter" Bitcoin, aiming to process transactions more quickly and cheaply. Dogecoin began as a joke, but the fun mascot and friendly image caught the internet's love making it widely recognized. All these altcoins try to improve on, or take a playful twist with the basic idea of digital money.

Today, altcoins are grouped into several main types, each with a special purpose or function.

Utility Tokens

Utility tokens are like special keys that unlock access to a network or technology. They are not only meant to represent value but also to power the systems built on top of blockchain. ETH (Ether), which runs the Ethereum network, is a utility token because users need ETH to pay fees when running smart contracts or moving assets around. Uniswap, a service for swapping tokens, relies on the same system. Instead of being simple payment coins, utility tokens enable apps and transactions that wouldn't work otherwise. Owning them is practical. You need them to use the network's services.

Stablecoins

Stablecoins pair the power of crypto with the predictability of traditional money. They are built for stability and convenience. These coins are usually tied to the value of a real-world asset, like the US dollar, so their price does not swing up and down like other cryptocurrencies. USD Coin (USDC) and Tether (USDT) are two big names in this category. People use stablecoins to move money across borders, settle trades, or protect their investments from price jumps. In daily use, you could consider stablecoins to be a digital version of cash that sits safely in your crypto wallet.

Meme Coins

Meme coins are crypto projects that start as jokes or online gags but sometimes grow huge because of community excitement. Dogecoin is the famous example. It was created in minutes, all for fun, and uses the Shiba Inu dog from an old internet meme as its mascot. Even without deep technical roots, meme coins can go viral, drawing crowds and attention. Yet, what makes them captivating is not their technology but the energy and unpredictability of their online fans. They often attract speculators who hope for big swings in value.

Privacy Coins

Privacy coins do what their name suggests: they shield the details of crypto transactions from public view. This focus on confidentiality can appeal to people who want to keep their financial moves private or live in places where digital freedom is threatened. Monero is a leading privacy coin, using special technology to hide both senders and amounts. Transactions on the Monero network cannot be traced like ones on Bitcoin or Ethereum. These coins offer a strong level of anonymity not found in most traditional payment systems.

Some altcoins are built for lasting value, supported by large teams, active communities, and real tools that people need. Others emerge and disappear primarily due to the influence of hype, rumors, jokes, or innovative ideas. Take Ethereum, for example: it powers NFT markets, decentralized finance apps, and whole networks of business activity. People use it every day to do things that are not possible with Bitcoin alone. On the other hand, a meme coin might rise in price just because of a social media event or celebrity tweet, with little behind it except for attention. While these coins can make headlines, their prices often swing wildly, and they rarely offer long-term solutions or uses beyond speculation.

To make the first steps into crypto investing, it helps to know what a coin actually does and who is building it. Coins with real software, well-managed teams, and active user groups are more likely to stick around. Meme coins and hot new tokens may be exciting, but they hold bigger risks. Some coins stand out for their technology or long-term vision, while others attract attention with bold promises or viral memes. For anyone interested in making their first investment, understanding what to look for becomes essential.

Evaluating and Identifying Promising Altcoins Safely

A clear process helps separate serious projects from the rest, but no single shortcut can cut through the altcoin hype. If you've learned to spot coins with empty buzzwords or those promising wild overnight riches, you're already moving in the right direction. The next step is putting practical steps into action, breaking down coins piece by piece to judge their real worth and risks.

Use Case: Understanding Real Purpose

Every altcoin should have a clear reason to exist. A strong coin usually solves a real problem, such as powering decentralized finance apps, speeding up international payments, or making online identities safer. If a project can't explain its purpose in simple terms, that's a sign to look closer.

Picture two coins: One supports a peer-to-peer lending app, showing how it helps users connect and borrow almost instantly, lowering fees and giving wider access. The other admits its only goal is to "go to the moon", a favorite meme phrase among joke coins. The first coin points to real-world use, while the second hides behind hype.

Ask questions like: Does this token unlock extra features in a service? Can it be used to pay for something, or does it only exist for trading? If answers are vague, or if the white paper feels padded with jargon and little substance, caution is warranted.

Team Assessment: Who's Behind the Coin?

Checking the team is like learning the chefs behind a new restaurant before you eat there. Great coins are built by transparent groups with proven records. Start by searching for developer or company profiles on the official website. Reputable teams list members by name, link to their social profiles, and often talk openly on platforms like Twitter, Discord, or Telegram.

Scan for clear project roadmaps. Honest projects lay out their future steps, what new features will drop, when updates will happen, and how security will improve. When a coin shares regular announcements, public meetings, or developer blogs, it's a strong reassurance.

On the flip side, if the website only mentions "expert developers," shows no photos, or uses first names only, ask yourself why. Anonymous creators, no matter how compelling their claims, raise risk.

Market Capitalization and Liquidity

Market capitalization is the total value of a coin's supply, calculated by multiplying the price by the number of coins in circulation. A high market cap often means a coin is more stable, and usually less likely to drop massively in value overnight. Bitcoin and Ethereum are leaders largely due to their size and trading volume.

Liquidity is just as crucial. It describes how easily you can buy or sell coins at a fair price. If there's little trading going on, you might be stuck holding coins no one else wants. Use platforms like CoinMarketCap to check daily trading volumes. If a coin has $50,000 traded each day and you want to sell $10,000, you're probably safe. If only $1,000 changes hands daily, it could be hard to exit your investment when you need to.

Adoption and Community Activity

A healthy coin shows steady growth and community involvement. Look for active development on code hosting sites like GitHub. Frequent software updates and open discussion among developers signal the project is alive and kicking. Strong social media engagement, clear announcements, and fast responses to user questions give even more assurance.

Watch for signals beyond numbers—partnerships with popular wallets, integrations with business platforms, or real usage statistics bolster confidence.

Signs of Growth

- Ongoing GitHub commits and updates
- Responsive and honest communication with users
- Partnerships or pilot programs with trusted companies
- Events, contests, and regular feedback opportunities

Recognizing Red Flags and Dangers

Rug Pulls

A "rug pull" happens when creators abandon a project after attracting large sums of money, often by yanking funds from the liquidity pool and leaving investors with worthless coins. Imagine a scenario: a new coin appears, hyped by influencers, prices skyrocket, and overnight the team's social channels go quiet. The coin's trading volume drops to almost nothing.

Patterns to watch out for:

- Hidden, anonymous, or unverified creators
- Smart contracts that haven't been audited or explained in public
- Claims of guaranteed massive returns
- Rushed launches without clear plans or documentation

Other Red Flags

Be alert if you notice:

- Vague, copy-and-pasted white papers
- Minimal communication from developers
- Reviewers flagging "locked" or unfairly distributed tokens
- Shocking price jumps caused by memes or viral tweets, not by updates or business wins

Practical Safety Strategies

Take cautious first steps by testing coins with small investments. Always use exchanges with a solid reputation for security and clear withdrawal processes. Double-check web addresses, bookmark official accounts, and follow reviews by trusted voices in crypto. Research using tools like CoinMarketCap for statistics or Etherscan to review smart contracts and token histories for transparency.

Investing a little more time upfront can prevent future headaches and financial losses.

Now that you understand what altcoins are, their different types, and how to carefully evaluate them, you're better equipped to navigate the exciting but sometimes confusing world of crypto. By focusing on coins with real purpose, strong teams, clear plans, and active communities, and by spotting warning signs early, you can make smarter choices that protect your investments from hype and scams. Remember, taking small, thoughtful steps rather than rushing in will build your confidence and help you discover digital assets that truly add value. With this foundation, you're ready to explore altcoins more safely and begin your journey toward informed, successful crypto investing.

CHAPTER 4
NFTS AND THE RISE OF DIGITAL OWNERSHIP

Imagine a world where owning a unique digital item is as straightforward and secure as holding a signed piece of art in your hands. This is the promise behind NFTs, or non-fungible tokens, a new form of digital ownership that's capturing headlines and opening fresh possibilities across art, gaming, and beyond. Unlike traditional money or cryptocurrencies, NFTs represent one-of-a-kind digital assets whose authenticity and ownership are recorded on a public blockchain, making forgery nearly impossible and ownership transparent.

In this chapter, we'll break down what NFTs really are, why they've gained so much attention, and how they work behind the scenes. You'll learn about their growing role in creative industries, gaming, and even digital identity, along with practical ways to evaluate NFTs if you're considering an investment. Whether you're curious about buying your first NFT or want to understand the risks and rewards of this new digital frontier, this chapter offers clear, accessible guidance to help you navigate the landscape with confidence.

Understanding NFTs: Definition, Popularity, and Crypto Context

Non-fungible tokens, also known as NFTs, provide a unique method to own digital assets. It helps to picture an NFT as a digital certificate of authenticity that proves a digital item is yours. While Bitcoin, dollars, or arcade tokens are interchangeable with each other, NFTs are not. For example, if you trade one dollar for another, you still have the same thing. An NFT works more like owning the signed original of a famous poster, while other people might have regular printouts or photos of that same poster.

What sets NFTs apart is their connection to the blockchain. The blockchain is like a public, tamper-proof record book that keeps track of who owns what, so you can't just copy and claim ownership of someone else's NFT. Each NFT has a unique digital signature, which can't be swapped exactly for another. This means an artist can publish a digital artwork as an NFT, and whoever buys it has the "official" copy. The NFT itself sits on the blockchain, while the image or video might be viewed by anyone, but only the NFT owner has blockchain-verified proof of ownership.

Many people get confused and think buying an NFT means you own the picture or video completely, like holding all the legal rights or stopping others from viewing it. That's not exactly true. If you buy a rare digital basketball trading card as an NFT, you might be able to display it or sell it, but you don't usually get the copyright or the right to prevent anyone else from looking at a screenshot of it online. Owning a signed comic book is akin to possessing a valuable original. While anyone can view pictures of it, only you possess the evidence that yours is the genuine item. An NFT is not the artwork itself. It's the digital proof of who owns the record of a specific version of that artwork on the blockchain.

Another big myth is that NFTs can be easily copied or faked. While you can copy the image or file, you can't clone the proof of ownership on the blockchain. The blockchain acts like a global notary office that everyone can check. If someone tries to sell a fake, the real NFT always points to the original record, making forgeries easy to spot. Some also imagine NFTs are just cryptocurrency or that they can be spent like Bitcoin or Ethereum. That's not the case. Cryptocurrencies are digital cash that can be sent, received, or spent, and each coin or token is the same. NFTs are unique items that run on some of the same technology, but they aren't spendable coins.

NFTs exploded in popularity for a mix of reasons. Celebrities and musicians began selling limited-edition songs and artwork as NFTs, which shot some headlines into the mainstream. In March 2021, a piece of digital art sold for $69 million, helping fuel worldwide interest. Video game companies let players trade NFT-based in-game items, like rare skins or weapons that you truly own, even outside the game. Sports fans started buying digital trading cards as NFTs. It also opened up a fresh path for artists and creators to earn money directly from fans, without sharing profits with big companies or galleries.

NFTs work using a process called "minting." To mint an NFT is to create a new, unique record on a blockchain. Most NFTs are minted on the Ethereum blockchain, but other blockchains support NFTs, too. After minting, the NFT exists as a digital token you can hold in a digital wallet. Think of this wallet like an app on your phone for your digital keys and assets. Smart contracts are short programs on the blockchain that manage these NFT transactions and guarantee you receive ownership, the seller gets paid, and even creators get a cut each time the NFT is resold. For example, somebody buying their first NFT might visit a marketplace, connect their wallet, pick a digital artwork, pay with cryptocurrency, and instantly get ownership recorded for them on the blockchain.

NFTs live alongside regular cryptocurrencies but fill a different role. Bitcoin and Ethereum are used for payment and as a kind of store of value, more like digital gold. NFTs use a similar "ledger" to record ownership but what you own is a specific digital thing, not a chunk of digital money. Both NFTs and cryptocurrencies require a wallet, can be bought and sold on digital marketplaces, and often live within the bigger world of decentralized apps, like DeFi lending platforms or new social networks.

Some NFTs are more than just collectibles or art. They play a role in new digital experiences like gaming, concert access, or proving your digital identity. As the uses keep expanding, NFTs are finding their way into new online adventures, which brings up questions about how they're used, how valuable they might be, and what risks come along with them. That's where the journey continues into the practical ways NFTs shape digital ownership, work as investments, and show up across industries beyond art and collectibles.

NFT Applications and Critical Evaluation for Investors

Walking through the expanding uses of NFTs unveils a world that blends creativity, identity, and social connection with a brand-new type of ownership. One of the first fields where NFTs made headlines was digital art. Artists who once struggled to earn a living online are now selling their work directly to fans as digital originals. Each NFT links to a single, unique piece of art stored and verified on a blockchain, like a digital signature proving both authenticity and ownership. For example, when Beeple sold his piece "Everydays: The First 5000 Days" as an NFT, it fetched millions and showed how digital artwork could be collected and traded with the same pride as a painting in a gallery. Collectors now browse platforms such as OpenSea, Rarible, or Foundation to discover works that come with verifiable histories and the sense of being the only official version in the world. But buying digital art also brings risks: images can be copied, artists may not always receive royalties, and high-profile sales attract imitators hoping to cash in.

NFTs have transformed gaming with a more interactive kind of ownership. In traditional games, players buy skins, weapons, or characters, but those items usually belong to the game company, not to the player. NFT-powered games flip that model. Assets such as swords, rare costumes, or even whole virtual land plots are minted as NFTs, which players can buy, sell, or trade as they wish. A positive example is Axie Infinity, a game where players breed, trade, and battle digital pets called Axies. Each Axie is an NFT on the blockchain, with its traits and value determined by rarity and demand. Players can earn, trade, or even lend their NFTs within the gaming community. This structure provides significant value to the time and money invested in the game, yet it presents both advantages and disadvantages. High upfront costs make some NFT games pay-to-play, and the market for in-game items can become a bubble, forcing latecomers to pay more for the same digital goods.

NFTs also play a growing role in digital identity and credentials. Rather than relying on usernames and passwords, people can use blockchain-powered certificates that prove who they are or what skills they've earned. For instance, a university might issue a diploma as an NFT, allowing employers to directly verify its origin and authenticity. Musicians and artists can launch membership passes as NFTs, granting owners exclusive access to live events, digital meet-ups, or special content. These tokens work like digital keys; if you own the right one, you're invited. This model is catching on with brands and content creators who want to reward loyal fans with early access or exclusive merchandise.

As NFT ownership expands, the investment question moves to the front of many minds. Some readers might wonder whether NFTs are the next big asset class, like Bitcoin or stocks. NFT markets have seen gigantic price swings. Some early buyers sold cartoon images or short clips for hundreds or thousands of times their purchase price. Yet prices can crash just as quickly, leaving others with assets they can't resell. A market full of excitement draws scammers and low-quality projects, making it challenging to pick a winner. Stories abound; some win life-changing profits by grabbing rare items early, while many more sink money into tokens that never sell again. The most successful NFTs tend to offer not only scarcity and eye-catching art but also strong communities, clear practical uses, and backing by recognizable artists or brands. Even then, holding an

NFT doesn't always mean you own the copyright or that you're protected from copycats.

Anyone thinking about buying or investing in NFTs should practice solid critical thinking and avoid buying based on hype. Here are important questions to ask before hitting "buy":

- Who is the creator or team behind the NFT? Do they have a reliable track record?
- What does the NFT offer the owner beyond the digital image or code? Does it include real-world perks, access, or future collaborations?
- Is the token rare, or will lots more be created, diluting its value?
- How active and supportive is the community around the project? Are other owners excited, engaged, and helping the project grow, or does it look abandoned?
- How easy is it to resell the NFT if you change your mind? Are there enough buyers, or is the market thin?
- Is the platform safe, and does it have protections against scams or sudden shutdowns?
- What rights do you actually receive? Owning the NFT doesn't always mean owning commercial rights to the artwork or using the asset however you want.

Looking past the headlines means checking real utility, active communities, proven creators, and platforms with a history of safe transactions. If an offer appears excessively favorable or appears hasty, it typically indicates a need to take a more measured approach. The best approach blends curiosity with healthy skepticism, aiming not for quick wins but for solid, informed decisions anchored in real value and lasting impact.

Now that we understand what NFTs are, why they matter, and how to evaluate them carefully, you're better equipped to navigate this fast-changing digital landscape with confidence. NFTs offer exciting possibilities, from owning unique art and in-game items to proving your identity and accessing exclusive experiences, but they also come with risks and complexities that demand thoughtful attention. By focusing on real value, trustworthy creators, and clear benefits rather than hype or quick profits, you can make smarter choices and avoid common pitfalls. As NFTs continue to grow and evolve, keeping a cautious but curious mindset will help you seize opportunities while protecting your investments in this new era of digital ownership.

CHAPTER 5

HOW TO BUY YOUR FIRST CRYPTO (STEP-BY-STEP)

"When I bought my first Bitcoin, I felt completely lost, like I had stumbled into a foreign country without a map," said one new investor. That feeling is common. The world of cryptocurrency can seem complicated and risky, especially for those who haven't dived into digital finance before. It's easy to worry about making mistakes or falling for scams when every step involves dealing with unfamiliar terms and websites. Yet, buying your first crypto doesn't have to be confusing or scary. With the right guidance, anyone can take this first step safely and confidently. This chapter offers practical insight designed just for beginners like you, helping you choose the right place to start, set up your account securely, and move forward with clarity rather than fear.

Selecting an Exchange and Creating Your Account

Cryptocurrency exchanges are the websites and apps that make it possible to buy, sell, and store digital currencies such as Bitcoin or Ethereum. Think of them as the digital shops where your crypto journey begins. Every beginner's first step is picking one of these "shops," and that choice matters for one clear reason: not all exchanges are equally safe, simple to use, or trustworthy. A solid platform protects your money and simplifies the learning process.

Some global exchanges you'll see mentioned often include Coinbase, Binance, and Kraken. These names have earned trust over years of operation, strict rules, and serving millions of users. Differences crop up when comparing them to smaller or offshore exchanges, which might have lighter regulation or be more vulnerable to hacks or sudden shutdowns. Highly regulated exchanges follow rules set by government bodies in places like the US or Europe. They offer a safety net for beginners because the law requires basic security and fair business practices.

Before making an account, you want to compare and check off a few must-have features for your own peace of mind.

What to Look For in a Good Exchange

Security

- Two-factor authentication (2FA) so you need a password *and* a code from your phone to log in or move funds
- Withdrawal whitelist features, letting you choose trusted wallet addresses and blocking others from draining your account
- Cold storage for customer money; most trusted exchanges keep most funds offline where hackers can't reach
- Solid track record with no major hacks or prompt, public reimbursement after any incident

A risky exchange lacks these features, uses only passwords, has been hacked with customer losses, or hides security details. On the other hand, a platform like Coinbase shows clear guides on enabling 2FA, describes insurance policies, and announces upgrades against new threats.

Reputation

- Look for industry awards, positive user reviews, and press coverage in major outlets
- Regulatory registration and a clear company history you can double-check
- No scandals, shutdowns, or reports of missing funds in the news or user forums

Imagine finding "Best Crypto Platform for Beginners" badges, a strong review score, and recent news articles describing steady growth. Compare that to an exchange with no press, angry comments, or a missing "about us" page.

Beginner-Friendliness

- Easy sign-up and clear navigation (large buttons, step-by-step help, transparent menus)
- Demo or "practice," modes for learning without risking money
- Chat or email support for new users guarantees a response within hours.
- Help sections should use simple language instead of confusing technical terms.

Popular exchanges often offer pop-up guides and even 24/7 chat teams, so getting stuck is rare.

To organize your choice, create a shortlist of three exchanges. Number them based on which seems safest and easiest after comparing criteria above. Double-check their features, reviews, and support before deciding which one to use.

How to Create Your Account, Step-by-Step

1. Open a browser or the app store and search for the exchange you chose. Make sure the URL starts with "https://" and shows a padlock icon. The padlock proves the website is secure.

Never click on links from emails or social media ads to avoid fake copycat websites.

2. Tap "Sign Up" and fill in your email and a *strong, unique* password. Never use old passwords reused anywhere else.

Weak: password123

Strong: Bx7$2mp9!cYE4qWz

Write your password down on paper or use a password manager.

3. After entering your email, check your inbox for a new message from the exchange. Click the link or enter the code sent to you. This step proves it's really you signing up.
4. The platform will guide you to upload documents for verification—a driver's license or passport photo, and maybe a quick selfie taken with your camera. This is required by law in many countries to prevent money laundering. Expect to wait a few minutes (or sometimes longer) while they confirm your ID. Double-check all your info matches exactly what's on your documents.

5. Once verified, set up two-factor authentication by linking your phone number or scanning a QR code with an authenticator app. Always enable this setting. It prevents anyone from logging in without your device.

Check every step before you hit "Submit." Turn on malware protection on your device and avoid doing this over public Wi-Fi.

Encouragement for Small Purchases

Many new investors start with $50 or even less. Every major exchange allows purchases as low as $1 to $10. This is a smart way to learn without overstretching. When you first log in, you may see a message like "Minimum first purchase: $5." It's normal, not a trick, and lets you get comfortable before making larger moves.

Completing registration and securing your account opens the door to your first buy. The steps you've just finished unlock every tool and setting you'll use to purchase crypto safely. Up next, you'll learn exactly how to fund your account and make your first investment with confidence.

Making Your First Purchase and Managing Security Settings

You have set up your exchange account and finished verification. The next steps bring you right to the heart of crypto: buying your first coins. When you log into your chosen exchange, focus on finding the area where purchases happen. The layout will look different depending on which exchange you use, but some patterns show up everywhere. On Coinbase, a blue "Buy/Sell" button sits on the top bar; this is your entry point. Binance has a "Buy Crypto" button right on the homepage, while Kraken's "Buy Crypto" link appears in the navigation menu. Look in the top menu, sidebar, or main dashboard for words like "Buy," "Trade," or "Markets." These are your signposts. If you don't see anything jumping out, try expanding the main dashboard menu since some platforms group all trading features together.

Once you enter the buy or trade screen, the exchange usually asks which cryptocurrency you want to buy. You might see a long list, a drop-down menu, or a search box. There are hundreds of coins out there, some with suspiciously similar names. Only buy large, reputable assets for your first purchase. For example, if you want Bitcoin, look for its official symbol, BTC. Ethereum is always ETH. Beware of coins with extra letters or odd punctuation - "BitcoinCash" is BCH (different from BTC), and "Ethereum Classic" is ETC (not ETH). If in doubt, check the exchange's information card, which almost always displays the coin's name and ticker symbol together.

Most exchanges make it easy to search. Start typing "Bitcoin" or "BTC" in the buy screen. The correct result usually pops up at the top, but always pause a second to look at the details. Stick with coins listed on the platform's main screen, as these go through a review before being offered. If you see a warning, low liquidity badge, or exclamation point, skip those for now.

After choosing your coin, the next step is deciding how much to buy. A simple field allows you to type in an amount in dollars or another local currency, or sometimes in the coin itself, such as 0.01 BTC. For beginners, start with a small, affordable amount that helps you get comfortable. You may see options for "Market Price" or "Limit Order." "Market Price" lets you buy instantly at the current rate, while a "Limit Order" allows you to set a preferred price and wait for the market to reach it. Limit orders can be confusing at first and are not necessary for your initial purchase, so stick with the market or instant option if available. If you see fields for payment methods or destination wallets, make sure the correct account or card is selected. Some platforms default to bank transfers, while others use linked debit cards.

Before confirming the purchase, you'll see a review screen. Exchanges typically display fees clearly, either as a dollar amount or a percentage. For example, on Coinbase, a $100 purchase may include a $2.99 fee, giving you about $97 worth of crypto. Most exchanges show this breakdown beneath your total. You will also notice purchase limits, since many platforms prevent you from buying less than a certain amount, such as $10, or more than your verified status allows. Avoid spending your entire balance on your first attempt, as digital coins can be volatile. A small purchase keeps the process low-pressure and helps you learn without stress.

Security is your lifeline. Enable two-factor authentication (2FA) before or immediately after your first purchase. This adds an extra layer of protection by combining your password with a code from your phone app or a text message. For instance, if someone steals your password, 2FA still prevents them from accessing your account. Never reuse old or simple passwords. Choose strong, unique ones that are not used elsewhere, and always use secure devices instead of public Wi-Fi.

After you click "Buy," you'll usually see a summary screen with your transaction details. The cryptocurrency amount may appear in your balance right away, especially for market orders, but sometimes the status shows "pending" while the payment clears. Some exchanges send an email receipt or a pop-up confirmation. Payments made by card tend to process faster than bank transfers, which can take a few hours or even longer for first-time buyers. If your crypto doesn't appear immediately, stay calm. Most delays last only a few minutes or a couple of hours, rarely more.

If something doesn't go as planned, you're not alone. A declined card, slow payment, or failed identity check can happen. Double-check your payment information, try a different card, or complete any verification steps in your profile. Minor issues, such as a "pending" status that lasts a bit longer than expected, rarely mean a loss. Contact customer support only if the delay continues or if an error message won't clear. Most exchanges want your business and are quick to resolve issues. Patience, along with steady, deliberate actions, keeps you in control.

Now that you've learned how to choose a trustworthy exchange and secure your account, you're ready to move forward with confidence. By taking practical steps like selecting a reliable platform, enabling strong security features, and starting with small purchases, you've built a solid foundation for your crypto journey. This careful approach helps you avoid common pitfalls and gives you full control. In the chapters ahead, you'll explore how to fund your account, make your first purchase, and manage your investments safely, all while deepening your understanding of this fast-evolving world without unnecessary risk or confusion.

CHAPTER 6

STORING YOUR CRYPTO SAFELY – WALLETS 101

More than 20% of all Bitcoin in existence has been lost or become inaccessible, often because people didn't take the right steps to protect their digital wallets. Unlike traditional money kept in banks, cryptocurrency exists entirely online, making it vulnerable to hackers, scams, and simple mistakes. Many new investors don't realize that where and how they store their crypto is just as important as buying it. Losing access to your funds isn't a matter of if, but when, unless you know how to keep them safe. This chapter will help you understand why securing your crypto matters and introduce the tools and methods that place control firmly in your hands.

Understanding Exchange Risks and Types of Crypto Wallets

Buying crypto is only the first step. Where you keep it determines whether you're truly in control of your money or exposed to outside risks. When coins remain on exchanges, the same platforms where you bought them, you give someone else power over your funds. It feels easy and familiar, like leaving your paychecks in a checking account. However, with crypto, exchanges can be surprisingly fragile.

Major exchanges have faced headline-making disasters that shattered trust across the industry. Consider the Mt. Gox collapse, where more than 800,000 Bitcoin disappeared overnight, leaving thousands of people locked out of their assets permanently. The Canadian platform QuadrigaCX met a similar fate when its founder died suddenly, and users soon discovered that hundreds of millions in coins were gone for good. These events may sound sensational, but they all stem from one problem: the risk of storing digital wealth in places beyond your control.

The key lesson is simple: "not your keys, not your coins." Imagine owning a house but giving the only key to a stranger. Every time you want to enter, you must wait for them to unlock the door. If something happens to them, or they choose to walk away, you lose access completely, no matter how much you trust them. Leaving crypto on exchanges requires a similar act of blind trust.

Take control of your security by understanding how crypto wallets work. A wallet in crypto isn't a place where coins physically sit. Instead, it's a digital tool that stores the credentials needed to access and move your funds on the blockchain. When you hold your own private keys, you are the only person who can decide how to use your assets. Every wallet allows you to receive, store, and send coins, but they fall into two main categories: hot and cold.

Hot wallets are software-based and connected to the internet. They come as browser extensions, phone apps, or desktop programs. They are quick and simple to set up, which makes them popular for beginners and everyday transactions. Apps such as MetaMask and Trust Wallet let you create a wallet and start sending or receiving crypto within minutes. The main advantage is convenience. If you use small amounts of crypto for regular purchases, a hot wallet functions like the wallet in your pocket, ready for coffee runs, online shopping, or small payments.

But being always connected to the internet is double-edged. Hot wallets are vulnerable to phishing, viruses, or hackers getting into your phone or computer. The same speed that makes these tools useful for fast access also poses a risk to users who store all their information online.

Ready for a sturdier option? Hardware wallets, also known as cold wallets, remain offline unless you choose to connect them. Devices such as Ledger Nano S, Ledger Nano X, and Trezor look like USB drives or small gadgets with screens. When you set one up, your private keys are created and stored securely inside the device. Only when you connect it to your computer to approve a transaction does your wallet interact with the internet, and even then, your private data never leaves the hardware. Think of a cold wallet as a safe deposit box at the bank. You use it to store your valuables long-term and only access them when you want to move a large amount.

Comparing the two makes the trade-offs clear. Hot wallets make spending easy but carry more day-to-day risk if you hold significant sums. Cold wallets provide stronger protection and peace of mind for long-term storage but are less convenient for frequent transactions.

Several misconceptions can trip up beginners. Some people believe all wallets offer the same level of security, but that is not true. Leaving your entire investment in a hot wallet or on an exchange creates open doors for thieves. On the other hand, hardware devices may look intimidating, but setting them up is straightforward and requires no advanced technical skills. Most popular hardware wallets guide you through the process with clear screens and step-by-step instructions. Think of it like buying a fireproof safe. You do not need to be a locksmith. You simply follow basic setup steps, record your backup code securely, and your valuables are protected.

Start by considering your habits and your comfort with risk. If you hold a small amount of crypto that you use regularly, a hot wallet is practical. For larger balances or assets you plan to hold long-term, dividing your funds between hot and cold storage is the safest approach. Keep only what you need for daily spending in a hot wallet, and store the rest securely in a hardware device.

Once you understand the basic types and what makes them safe, the next question is: how do you pick the right wallet and avoid mistakes that could lose your funds? You'll want to know how to create backups, where and how to hide your recovery phrases, and ways to spot fake software. These first steps pave the way for securing your crypto with real confidence, never relying on luck or hope alone.

Choosing the Right Wallet and Protecting Your Assets

Understanding the differences between hot and cold wallets sets the stage for what really matters: making sure your crypto stays safe as you use it day by day. After learning about storage types, the next real question is what fits your needs and routines. Security isn't just an abstract worry. Once you hold digital assets, even small amounts, your focus shifts to practical control, seeing your assets available but protected from theft, mistakes, or gadget failures.

Matching Wallets to Real-Life Habits

A wallet is not a universally applicable tool. Your ideal choice depends on how you use your crypto. If you want a simple way to access and manage tokens for daily use, you may lean toward an app or browser extension. If your main focus is security and you plan to hold rather than trade often, physical devices make more sense.

MetaMask

MetaMask is a software wallet that works as a browser extension or mobile app. It's a favorite for new users who want to interact with decentralized apps or buy, store, and send Ethereum and similar tokens. Setting up MetaMask begins with a simple app installation. Once inside, friendly prompts and visual cues guide you. You'll see current balances, recent transactions, and ways to connect to trading sites or apps, all in one place.

For someone buying crypto for the first time, MetaMask can hold small amounts for regular use, like buying an NFT or swapping coins. The main draw is ease: install, follow the prompts, and you're ready to interact. Still, MetaMask's convenience means your assets are only as safe as your device. If you use MetaMask on a laptop or phone, malware or theft can reach your wallet unless you take extra care.

Ledger

Ledger is a hardware wallet, a physical device that stores your private keys offline. The most popular models look like small USB drives. To set it up, you connect it to a computer, walk through step-by-step screens, and write down a recovery phrase. Ledger's real advantage is security. Since your keys never touch the internet, they stay protected from hackers, even if your computer is infected.

For those building a crypto nest egg or holding coins for months or years, Ledger shifts control to you. Think of it like a home safe: no one can access it unless they hold the device and the recovery phrase. There is a learning curve, plugging in, using the app, and following instructions to approve each action, but it becomes routine with practice. Someone holding Bitcoin for the long haul may move large amounts to Ledger for peace of mind and only remove assets when needed.

Trust Wallet

Trust Wallet is a mobile app tailored for broad crypto support. It allows users to buy, store, swap, and stake a wide range of coins from their phone. Beginners find Trust Wallet friendly due to its clean interface and strong cheat sheets guiding setup. Imagine a person on the go, wanting to manage collectibles, sign into games, or keep daily spending money handy; Trust Wallet offers that flexibility.

Compared with MetaMask or Ledger, Trust Wallet sits in the middle. It's more secure than a browser alone but not as protected as a device kept offline. The main tradeoff is between ease of access and the risk if your phone is lost or breached.

Protective Habits for All Wallets

Choosing a wallet is step one. Keeping it safe makes all the difference. Start with creating secure passwords for every app and device, using a mix of random letters, numbers, and symbols. Never use names, birthdays, or words someone could guess. If your wallet app offers two-factor authentication (2FA), always enable it. 2FA asks for a code from your phone or another app when signing in, blocking intruders even if they steal your password.

Next, generate and save your seed phrase, 12 or 24 random words that unlock your wallet from any device. Write these down on paper, not on your phone, not in emails, and never in cloud storage. Some people make the mistake of screenshotting their phrase or sending it to themselves via chat. This exposes funds to anyone who hacks the account. Instead, keep the paper hidden somewhere only you can reach.

Backup matters too. Store wallet details and recovery phrases in a secure box or safe. Tell only one trusted person where this backup exists, in case of accidents. Never type private keys or seed phrases into unknown websites or support chat windows. Only enter them during wallet setup, and only through the official app or device.

Take a moment before using any wallet app. Check you're using the real one, not a fake. On hardware wallets, verify the device is genuine and behaves as expected. Scammers use fake apps and phishing to steal coins.

Losing a device doesn't mean losing assets if you have your seed phrase. You can restore your wallet on a new phone or hardware device using the backup. Without those recovery words, even the company behind the wallet cannot get your funds back. Treat this information like your own digital bank vault.

Making these safety measures habits reduces anxiety and puts you firmly in control. Handling crypto gets smoother when you build security into your daily life. Each step, from choosing a wallet to storing backup phrases, fits into a pattern of awareness and care that anyone can learn.

Now that you understand the critical importance of securely storing your cryptocurrency and the practical ways to protect your assets, you're ready to take control with confidence. Whether you choose a hot wallet for everyday convenience or a cold wallet for long-term safety, the key is matching your tools to your habits and risk level. By adopting good security practices, like safeguarding your seed phrase, using strong passwords, and verifying your wallet apps, you can avoid common pitfalls and keep your digital wealth truly yours. With these foundations in place, you're prepared to navigate the crypto world safely, turning curiosity into smart, secure investing.

CHAPTER 7
HOW TO BUILD A SMART, SIMPLE CRYPTO PORTFOLIO

Emma clicked through her crypto wallet, heart pounding as she stared at dozens of coins she'd bought over the past few months. Each one promised huge returns—tweets, forums, and flashy headlines had pulled her deeper into a world she barely understood. Yet instead of feeling excited, she felt overwhelmed, confused by the sheer number of assets and news to track. Every day seemed like a gamble, and the fear of missing out pushed her to buy more, even when she didn't fully grasp what she owned.

If you've ever found yourself in Emma's shoes, wondering how to balance hope for growth with caution, you're not alone. Many new investors jump in thinking success means owning every popular coin or chasing the next big thing. But that approach can lead to stress, confusion, and losses, making it harder to build real confidence or steady gains.

This chapter steps back from the chaos to show how keeping your crypto portfolio smart and simple can make all the difference. You'll see why focusing on a few solid choices, not dozens, helps protect your money and your peace of mind. Whether you want slow, steady growth or are curious about reaching for bigger wins without losing sleep, there's a way to create a plan that fits your comfort level and goals.

Before investing, learn the value of simplicity and strategy in the fast-paced crypto world. This isn't about hype or rushing; it's about building a thoughtful foundation that sets you up to learn, grow, and invest smarter over time.

Understanding Portfolio Simplicity and Sample Beginner Portfolios

Think of your crypto portfolio like a grocery basket. You wouldn't grab everything in the shop, you'd get the basics, maybe something new you've researched, and skip what feels too strange or risky. In crypto, there's a common myth that real success comes from owning a slice of everything or filling your digital wallet with as many coins as you can. The truth is, especially for someone just starting out, a few well-chosen coins bring more control, less stress, and a much safer journey.

Spreading money over too many coins turns portfolio management into a guessing game. With so many projects launching and social media hype running wild, it's easy to believe you're missing out if you're not constantly adding new tokens. But holding every new coin or trendy project means you're less likely to understand the details of what you actually own. This brings a hidden risk: some lesser-known coins can crash hard, lose value overnight, or even disappear. Chasing every opportunity often leads to more confusion and bigger losses than steady progress.

Simplicity also protects your time and peace of mind. Just as most people wouldn't buy every stock on the market, you don't need to fill your crypto portfolio with dozens of coins. The more coins you have, the more difficult it becomes to track performance, spot risks, and keep up with news and security measures for each asset. Focusing on a handful of coins means you can actually follow what's happening, learn how they behave during market swings, and make smarter decisions when it matters most.

Building around a few leading assets makes you less likely to end up with "dead weight" in your portfolio; those coins that sit forgotten, performing poorly while eating up space and money. Sticking to a simple, thoughtful mix keeps things easy to monitor. This gives you space to build confidence at your pace, without being pulled in a thousand directions.

Sample Beginner Portfolios by Risk Tolerance

Pick a portfolio based on how much risk makes sense for your life and your goals. Here's what that looks like in practice, with three sample strategies:

Conservative Portfolio

A conservative portfolio means putting most of your money into the oldest, most established coins. These assets have the longest track records and the strongest reputations for surviving price drops and market trouble. For a simple option:

- **Bitcoin:** 60%
- **Ethereum:** 35%
- **USDC (a leading stablecoin):** 5%

This is for someone like Sarah, who wants steady growth and doesn't want many surprises. She checks her account a few times a month rather than every day and likes knowing her money is in coins that the whole industry watches closely. Her goal is gradual wealth-building over several years, not quick profits.

Balanced Portfolio

A balanced portfolio shares funds between big-name coins and a small slice of promising alternatives. It suits people who want to capture more upside but prefer to keep most of their money in safer bets. An example split:

- **Bitcoin:** 50%
- **Ethereum:** 30%
- **Cardano or Solana:** 15%
- **USDC:** 5%

Imagine Justin, who's curious enough to research new technologies but still needs stability. He's comfortable reading up on news about his top coins and likes having one pick outside the top two for new growth. His ambition is to grow his money faster than a savings account while avoiding the high drama of riskier portfolios.

Aggressive Portfolio

An aggressive portfolio leans hard into emerging coins with the hope of higher returns and accepts the swings that come with that. Here's a setup for the bold:

- **Bitcoin:** 40%
- **Ethereum:** 25%
- **Solana:** 10%
- **Polygon:** 10%
- **Small-Cap Coin:** 10%
- **USDC:** 5%

Jenny, for instance, wants a shot at bigger gains and likes hunting for the next breakout star. She spends time researching new crypto projects, follows developers on social media, and is fine with value jumping up and down. What drives her is potential upside, but she understands this brings periods of losses along the way.

Matching Your Approach

The best fit depends on how hands-on you want to be and how much you can handle watching prices move around. Ask yourself:

- Do I want quiet, long-term growth or the chance for faster wins and losses?
- Am I willing to spend time keeping up with new projects and news?
- Will big swings in value make me anxious, or are they part of the thrill?

Pick a structure that leaves you sleeping well at night, not staring at charts at 2 a.m. Don't copy someone else's choices. Your mix should match your personal feeling about risk, time, and learning style.

Now that you've seen what a focused portfolio looks like, the big questions become about how to split your money, balance coins, and keep things working over time. This is where strategy comes to life, and your blueprint for safe, practical investing really begins to take shape.

Allocating, Diversifying, and Maintaining Your Crypto Portfolio

Building on earlier portfolio templates, it's time to turn those ideas into reality. Many new investors think success means owning dozens of coins, but picking just a few solid choices and sticking to a clear plan can be safer and less stressful. Three big skills - allocation, diversification, and rebalancing make those plans easier to follow.

Allocation: How much should I put where?

Allocation means deciding how much money you'll put into each crypto asset. Instead of jumping in and buying whatever looks hot, you take your total investment amount and make a careful plan.

Let's say you have $1,000 saved for this goal. You might decide on a split like

- 60% Bitcoin (BTC) = $600
- 30% Ethereum (ETH) = $300
- 10% Solana (SOL) = $100

A safer, lower-risk style might use 80% in BTC, 15% in ETH, and only 5% in an altcoin. Risk-tolerant investors might go the other way, but beginners should remember: more money in the older, bigger coins gives you a cushion if prices swing.

Why think about allocation so seriously? Writing down your plan helps you avoid the urge to chase big winners or dump everything when prices fall. Those clear boundaries make it less likely you'll panic during the next market dip. Whenever you add more money to your portfolio, use your chosen percentages again to keep things simple.

Diversification: Don't put all your eggs in one basket

Diversification protects you from the risk that one coin performs badly while another does well. Instead of betting on a single asset, you spread your investment over several. For example, suppose your portfolio is 100% BTC. If BTC drops 40% in a few months, your entire investment falls by 40%. But if your allocation is 50% BTC, 40% ETH, and 10% SOL, and during a tough season BTC drops 40%, ETH holds steady, and SOL rises 20%, your losses are softened.

Here's a simple way to think about it:

- If one asset is down, others might be stable
- Winners and losers often take turns
- Keeping three to five coins avoids confusion
- More coins aren't always better; just one or two will pose more risk than a balanced basket

Sticking to a handful of familiar, trusted coins protects you from hype and hidden dangers. For most beginners, starting with BTC, ETH, and one or two more is both practical and smart.

Rebalancing: Check and adjust your plan

Markets move, and so will the value of the assets you own. Over time, one coin might double while another drifts down. Your portfolio could drift from your original plan. This is where rebalancing comes in. Rebalancing means checking regularly to see if your allocations still match your target percentages. If they don't, you sell some of what's grown and buy what's lagged until things are back in line.

Here's a simple checklist:

- Pick a schedule (every 3 or 6 months)
- Review your coin values and amounts
- Compare to your original percentage plan
- Sell a portion of coins that grew above target
- Buy coins that slipped below target

Example

Suppose your target is 60% BTC, 30% ETH, 10% SOL. After three months, BTC soared to 70% of your portfolio. You'd sell part of your BTC and shift that money to ETH or SOL to restore your original balance. This routine keeps your risk level from drifting up without your noticing.

Dollar-Cost Averaging (DCA): A steadier approach to buying

Dollar-cost averaging (DCA) is a process where you invest set amounts (say $100) at regular intervals (like monthly), instead of trying to guess the perfect time to buy. Some months prices will be higher, some lower, and your buying average smooths out over time.

Picture a six-month scenario:

- Month 1: $100 at $30,000 (BTC)
- Month 2: $100 at $32,000
- Month 3: $100 at $28,000
- Month 4: $100 at $25,000
- Month 5: $100 at $26,000
- Month 6: $100 at $31,000

Your average buy price comes out much lower than if you'd poured in $600 all at once during a price spike. DCA keeps you from stressing over day-to-day moves and lets you stay in the game steadily.

Long-term thinking: Patience beats panic

Short-term volatility in crypto can trigger big emotional swings. When prices fall, the urge to sell and "cut losses" is strong. But history shows that most people who hold quality coins through downturns tend to recover and often come out ahead. For instance, someone who bought BTC during its all-time high in 2017 and held through the deep 2018 crash still saw the value multiply by 2021. Someone else who panicked and sold early missed out.

illustration:

Year	BTC Price
2017	$19,000
2018	$6,000

Sticking to a clear plan, rebalancing regularly, and keeping a long-term mindset can help protect your investments and your peace of mind.

Now that you understand how to build a simple, balanced cryptocurrency portfolio tailored to your comfort with risk and time, you're ready to take practical steps toward smart investing. Keeping your focus on a few well-chosen coins helps you stay in control, avoid common pitfalls, and grow your confidence as you learn more about this exciting space. By planning your allocation, diversifying thoughtfully, rebalancing regularly, and embracing patience, you create a strong foundation that can weather the ups and downs of crypto markets. With these tools in hand, you can move forward with clarity and calm, turning your curiosity into steady, informed action on your journey to building digital wealth.

CHAPTER 8

UNDERSTANDING RISK (AND HOW TO AVOID LOSING IT ALL)

Did you know that the value of many cryptocurrencies can swing by double digits within just a few hours? Unlike traditional markets that close for the day, crypto trades nonstop, leading to rapid and often unexpected price changes. These wild ups and downs can make investing in digital currencies feel like riding a rollercoaster without a seatbelt. Understanding why these shifts happen and how emotions influence decisions is key to protecting your money. This chapter will guide you through the nature of cryptocurrency risk and offer practical ways to keep control, even when the market feels unpredictable.

Decoding Crypto Volatility and Investor Emotions

Cryptocurrency prices can jump or crash in what feels like the blink of an eye. Unlike traditional stock markets that follow business hours, crypto trading happens every hour of every day, and anyone in the world can join in. This means prices are always moving, sometimes in big, unpredictable ways. Many of these wild swings happen because the market is still fairly new. Bitcoin, for example, only launched in 2009, so compared to stocks or gold, its "track record" is quite short. Most cryptocurrencies have even less history, leaving investors with fewer data points to feel steady about.

Another reason for big price jumps is the size of the market itself. The total value of all cryptocurrencies is much smaller than traditional financial markets. In a smaller market, even a few people moving money in or out can make a big difference in price. Picture a seesaw on a playground: if only one or two people climb on, it teeters quickly. Crypto's playground works in a similar way. Because crypto assets are traded all over the world, any big piece of news or sudden action from a large investor, sometimes called a "whale", can tip the market fast. If someone with a giant stash of bitcoin decides to sell, the whole price can drop suddenly, catching smaller investors off guard.

News stories and social media posts spark quick reactions, too. A single celebrity tweet or a government regulation announcement can send prices soaring or crashing almost instantly. For example, when a famous entrepreneur once tweeted support for Bitcoin, the price shot up in minutes. But when the same person later expressed doubts, prices dipped just as fast. In another case, when a country's government announced a possible ban on crypto, panic spread and led to a steep sell-off. These types of dramatic rises and falls are called volatility. Some people see chances to make money in these swings, but for newcomers, it often feels confusing or worrying.

There are solid ways to hold steady even when the market looks like a rollercoaster. The first trick is to decide ahead of time how much you can afford to invest and only use money you could lose without it hurting your life. This way, big price drops won't put you in real trouble. Many smart investors also spread their money across more than one kind of crypto or even keep some in regular savings, so if one coin crashes, they still have something left. Setting clear rules for when to buy or sell, rather than acting on a whim, makes panic less likely.

It helps to look at the long road, not just today's price. Crypto often bounces up and down in the short term, but steps upward and downward shape long-term trends. Some people call this approach HODLing, which means holding onto your investment even during storms. For example, an investor who bought bitcoin a few years ago might have watched its price drop by half in just a week. Some people sold everything in fear, but this person waited patiently until the price recovered and even climbed above their original buying point.

When chaos strikes, it's tempting to follow rumors or invest in the newest tip. By sticking with your original plan and ignoring daily drama, you let the odds work for you over time. A simple checklist helps: before making any move, ask yourself if this fits your plan or if you're just reacting to headlines or a friend's advice.

Emotions push people to make choices they later regret. FOMO, or "fear of missing out," happens when you see prices rising and want to buy in so you don't miss gains, even if you haven't researched the project. Greed urges people to chase quick profits, buying when prices are already high in hopes of more. Panic selling occurs when prices decline, fear overwhelms, and individuals rush to sell, often resulting in significant losses. These feelings are normal, but they can make you act against your interest.

To sidestep these emotional traps, write down your reasons for every investment. If you set a goal like selling if your coin rises 30% or only investing a set amount stick with it. When headlines start to worry you, read your journal and remember how you made those choices. By noticing your own feelings, you can stop yourself from trading impulsively and focus on steady growth.

Learning how crypto markets twist and turn, and understanding your own reactions, gives you a guidebook for calmer investing. Beyond these basics, you'll need smart ways to keep your risk low, not just to avoid losing money, but to spot trouble before it starts. The next parts will break down clear strategies for safer investing so you can act confidently no matter what the markets throw your way.

Beginner Risk Management and Avoiding Costly Mistakes

Everyone feels the pull of excitement when crypto prices soar or a friend brags about huge gains. That buzz of possibility isn't just emotional; it can cloud judgment and put beginner investors in harm's way. One minute you're curious, the next you're feeling FOMO and hitting "buy" based on a hot tip. This emotional rollercoaster mixes with genuine complexity, creating a setting where mistakes and scams can sneak up fast. The secret is turning that anxious energy into action. Risk can't be erased, but it can be managed.

Practical Risk Management Techniques

Basic steps lay the groundwork for safer investing. Security comes first. Use a strong password for every crypto account, mixing letters, numbers, and symbols, and never repeat passwords. Two-factor authentication (2FA) adds another wall between your assets and intruders. With 2FA, even if someone steals your password, they still need a code from your phone or another secure device. For the most secure storage, hardware wallets keep crypto offline, protecting it from internet hacks. These are tiny devices like USB sticks, if they're not plugged in, your assets are unreachable through cyberattacks.

Solid portfolio habits matter just as much. Never invest money you depend on for rent, groceries, or emergencies. Crypto's price swings are unpredictable, you might see deep drops within days. Instead, decide the total amount you're comfortable losing entirely, and treat that as your upper limit. Diversification means spreading your investment across several coins or tokens to avoid heavy damage if one crashes. If you buy only one currency and it tanks, your whole portfolio suffers.

Taking profits on the way up helps sidestep regret. Suppose you buy a coin for $500, it doubles, and you sell half your holdings. Even if the price falls afterward, you've already taken gains and protected

your original funds. Stop-loss orders can limit disaster by selling automatically if a price dips past your chosen threshold. For example, you set a stop-loss at 15% below your buy price. If the market tumbles, your assets get sold before you lose much more.

When prices jump after you invest, resist the urge to "chase" and keep pouring in more. Hype often fades as quickly as it arrived, and newcomers can be left with big losses while earlier sellers cash out. Take time to check facts and reflect instead of acting on emotion.

Common Crypto Scams and Clear Warning Signs

The crypto world is full of shortcuts and traps. Pump-and-dump schemes are one of the oldest tricks. Imagine an online chat group suddenly claims a little-known coin will skyrocket. People rush in, the price jumps, then the original promoters dump their holdings, causing the price to collapse. Newcomers buy at the top, then watch their investment evaporate.

Fake tokens and knockoff coins often come with slick names or websites that look almost real. A beginner sees "Ethereum Plus," thinks it's connected with Ethereum, and sends their funds. The project vanishes a few weeks later.

Phishing is everywhere. You might get an email or message that seems to come from your exchange or wallet provider, urging you to act fast and click a link. The link leads to a site that looks just like the real thing, when you log in, scammers snag your password and empty your account.

Ponzi and pyramid schemes pop up, promising sky-high returns if you recruit others or lock in your coins. Someone you know insists they're making easy money and offers you a spot, but payments only last until new investors run out. The scheme collapses, leaving most with nothing.

Fraudulent giveaways on social media are common. A fake "celebrity" account might ask you to send one coin to get two back. Once you send your crypto, it's gone.

Spotting the Red Flags

- Promises of guaranteed, outsized returns
- Urgent messages pushing you to act right away
- Requests for your private key or recovery phrase
- Websites with spelling errors, clunky layouts, or missing information
- Investments with complicated structures that aren't clearly explained
- Messages from unknown contacts insisting on secrecy or pressure

Default to caution. If something feels off, pause and double-check. Trust builds slowly, but one careless click can undo months of effort.

Avoiding Rookie Mistakes That Cause Big Losses

Anonymous projects that promise significant breakthroughs can easily capture your attention. Many rug pulls begin this way; the creators vanish, and the project's funds disappear with them. Always google the project, scan crypto forums, and look for real names and team information.

Sending crypto to the wrong address is a classic error. Transactions are irreversible. Always copy and paste wallet addresses, check the first and last few characters, and send a small test amount before transferring larger sums.

Impatience trips up many beginners. Trying to buy the dip or catch the peak, people end up buying high and selling low. Automated alerts or reminders can help dampen the urge to act quickly.

Stored funds on exchanges are an easy target for hacks. Move long-term assets into secure wallets instead of leaving them online.

Chasing every new token burns through funds. Instead, start with small amounts, set clear goals for each investment, and stick to them.

Every year brings headlines of people losing life savings after sending crypto to scammers or betting on anonymous projects that disappear. Prevention starts with routine checks, steady habits, and a cool head. Protection isn't about technical tricks; it's about common sense, preparation, and knowing that you're always one step ahead when you choose caution over speed.

Now that we've unpacked the wild ups and downs of cryptocurrency, the emotional traps investors face, and practical ways to protect your money, you're better prepared to step into this fast-moving world with confidence. By understanding what drives crypto prices, managing your risk wisely, and spotting scams before they catch you off guard, you set yourself up for smarter choices and steadier progress. Remember, successful investing isn't about chasing every trend or reacting to every headline; it's about sticking to a clear plan, staying calm when markets shake, and learning as you go. With these tools in hand, you're ready to take the next steps toward building your crypto portfolio safely and thoughtfully.

CHAPTER 9
MAKING PASSIVE INCOME WITH CRYPTO

Just a few years ago, the idea of earning money from cryptocurrencies without actively trading or constantly monitoring markets was something only tech experts discussed. Fast forward to today, and passive income streams in crypto are now available to everyday people who want to build wealth without diving into complex charts or taking major risks.

As exciting as this sounds, the world of passive crypto earnings is full of choices and challenges that can feel overwhelming. How do you know which options are safe? Which opportunities are real, and which might be too good to be true?

This chapter explores the practical side of making your crypto work for you quietly in the background. It will show you how to approach these methods with a clear understanding of both the potential rewards and the hidden risks. The goal is to find steady, reliable ways to grow your digital assets while keeping control and caution at the forefront.

Understanding Passive Crypto Income Methods and Platforms

Stepping into the world of passive income with crypto can feel like entering a maze of new faces, buzzwords, and tempting promises. The good news is you don't need to be an expert or a day trader to earn reliable, ongoing returns. Three of the most popular, and approachable, passive income methods are staking, yield farming, and liquidity pools. With the right guidance, these can offer steady rewards in exchange for helping to maintain the systems that power crypto.

Staking: Earning Rewards the Safe Way

Staking is one of the simplest ways to earn passive crypto income. Certain blockchains need people to lock up their tokens to help run the network safely and process transactions. Anyone who owns these tokens can "stake" them, basically, let the network use them for a while. In return, you earn rewards as a thank you from the network itself.

Here's how staking might work for a beginner:

Imagine you have some ADA (the coin for the Cardano blockchain). You want to earn more ADA without selling or trading. You look for a staking option on your exchange, decide how much ADA to lock up, and follow three easy steps:

1. Select "Stake" in your crypto wallet or exchange.
2. Choose the amount to stake and confirm.
3. Wait while your ADA is staked for a certain period.

Every few days or weeks, you'll see a bit of extra ADA appear in your account as a reward. If you decide to unstake, you might have to wait a few days before you can spend or move your coins again. Rewards can vary, but the process is designed so you don't need to supervise it. Many newcomers choose staking because it's

straightforward and doesn't require special knowledge or equipment.

Yield Farming: Chasing Higher, Variable Returns

Yield farming can sound a little wild, but the core idea is simple. You lend your crypto or place it somewhere others can borrow or swap, then collect a share of the profits the platform makes. The keyword here is "yield", your earnings can change, and there's a bit more going on behind the curtain.

Suppose you decide to try yield farming on a platform using USDT (a stablecoin pegged to the US dollar). The process might look like this:

1. Move your USDT to a DeFi protocol's wallet.
2. Choose a lending pool or a yield farm.
3. Deposit your USDT.

Other users borrow your USDT, paying fees or interest to the protocol. The platform shares those profits with you, so your earnings can go up and down depending on activity. Yield farming often offers higher possible returns than staking, but you need to pay closer attention—yields can drop, the protocol could run into trouble, or interest rates can change unexpectedly.

Liquidity Pools: Powering Decentralized Trading

Liquidity pools are shared baskets of crypto that make it possible for people to swap tokens without needing buyers or sellers lined up all the time. Anyone can add assets to these pools, usually on a DeFi platform. By doing so, you help others trade with ease and get paid a slice of trading fees when swaps happen.

Here's a relatable example:

You hold both ETH and USDC and put the same value of each into an ETH/USDC liquidity pool. The pool uses your crypto (and others' too), so when someone trades ETH for USDC, there's always enough of each. For helping, you get a share of the fees from each trade. Your role is like being a mini-bank that always offers cash on hand. Liquidity pools can handle big sums, but for beginners, many platforms offer guides and calculators so you can estimate your rewards.

Centralized vs. Decentralized Platforms

Where you use these strategies has a big effect on your comfort and security. Centralized exchanges (CEX), like Coinbase or Binance, work a lot like regular banks. They hold your crypto for you, offer easy-to-use menus, and often have solid customer support. You just click "stake," and it happens in the background. The downside is you give up a bit of control, and if the platform has issues, you might not have a quick way out.

DeFi platforms, by contrast, put all the power and responsibility in your hands. You hold your wallet, make every decision, and see all the transactions "on chain." You can get more rewards, and there's no bank, but if you lose your keys or make a mistake, you're on your own. Since DeFi is open to everyone, you must be vigilant against scams and bad actors.

Weighing the Choices

Choosing the right passive income method depends on your goals and your appetite for risk. it's familiar, and there's usually quick support. If you're more adventurous and want to dig deeper, DeFi options like yield farming or liquidity pools can pay more, but you'll need to do your homework on platform safety, understand the possible swings in earnings, and keep track of your crypto security.

These income streams look promising, but it's smart to explore deeper before locking up your assets. The next step is to look at what shapes safety and returns, making sure your path is both rewarding and secure.

Evaluating APY, Risks, and Safety Before Investing

When you hear about people making passive income with crypto, the numbers can sound eye-popping. A website might promise an APY of 100%, 500%, or even 1000% if you deposit your coins into their pool or farm. APY, or annual percentage yield, is just a fancy way of saying how much your money might earn if you keep it locked up for a full year. If you deposit $1,000 somewhere that offers a 100% APY, the claim is that you'd have $2,000 after 12 months. This sounds exciting, but there's a catch: high APY often means high risk, sometimes even danger to your original funds.

To understand this, picture two banks. One is old, reliable, and offers modest interest. The other is brand new with neon signs, offering to double your money in a year. In the real world, that second bank would make you suspicious. Crypto works in much the same way. High APYs attract attention, just like get-rich-quick schemes you might have seen before, but rarely are these offers as smooth as they appear.

Platforms achieve these big numbers with risky projects or by giving you tokens that might not be worth much in the future. Imagine depositing money to earn rewards in a token you've never heard of, only to watch its value drop to almost nothing overnight. These types of losses may occur when a project's token lacks strong demand or when team members abuse their authority to create additional tokens arbitrarily.

There are more dangers. Some high APY pools can be outright scams. You might have heard terms like "rug pull," where the team running a project drains all the money and disappears. Other times, the platform might seem legitimate, but it turns out the team is anonymous. If no one knows who is behind the project, you have no way to hold them accountable. Real projects usually have a public team with clear social media profiles and a record of communicating with users.

Market swings can wipe out your gains. Say you join a pool with a 40% APY, but the price of the token you're rewarded with drops 90% during the year. Even after getting all your rewards, you might end up with less than you started. There's also a thing called liquidity risk. If everyone rushes to take out their money at once, the platform might freeze withdrawals, leaving you unable to move your coins. You'd be stuck and possibly watching your balance go down in value.

If a platform offers incredible rewards, always check how long it's been around. Crypto moves fast, but projects that have lasted at least a year and survived ups and downs often show they're more solid. Look for security audits. These are like financial health checkups for the code that runs the platform. You'll usually see these mentioned on the project's website or blog if they exist. Good platforms work with outside companies to review their smart contracts, then publish those results.

Before trusting a platform, try searching its name with the word "scam" or "review." See what other users say in forums or on social media. A solid reputation almost always leaves a trail of real reviews, honest complaints, and helpful advice. If you are unable to find much information about a platform, or if red flags consistently appear, consider it a warning sign.

Always start with a small amount. Treat your first deposit as an experiment. Watch what happens. Does the platform do what it promised? Is it easy to withdraw? If even a tiny test leaves you waiting for your money or confused by hidden rules, imagine how much more stressful it would be with serious funds at stake.

Understanding a few extra ideas helps you play safer. Liquidity pools and yield farms come with something called impermanent loss, where the value of your deposits can change in ways you don't expect if prices move a lot. Withdrawal delays or time-locks can keep you from getting your cash out when you need it. Smart contract risk means that bugs in the platform's computer code could drain the pool or freeze your funds permanently.

Here, a classic rule applies: if a crypto project promises returns that appear excessively high, they almost always are. Take time to read guides, learn basic terms, and ask questions. Slow, steady earning in crypto often beats jumping for the shiniest deal, helping you avoid costly mistakes and keep your learning journey on solid footing.

Now that you understand the main ways to earn passive income with crypto and the vital safety checks to keep your money secure, you're better equipped to start your journey wisely. Whether you choose the simplicity of staking or the higher potential rewards of yield farming and liquidity pools, remember that patience, research, and caution are your best tools. By taking small steps, verifying platforms, and staying aware of risks like scams or market swings, you can build a solid foundation for earning in this exciting space. With this knowledge, you're ready to explore opportunities confidently, setting yourself up not just to chase quick gains, but to grow your crypto steadily and securely over time.

CHAPTER 10
TAXES, REGULATIONS, AND WHAT TO WATCH FOR

Have you ever wondered what really happens behind the scenes when you buy or sell cryptocurrency? Or why some transactions seem simple while others come with surprises such as extra paperwork or unexpected fees? How do governments track digital money that is not printed or controlled by banks?

These questions can leave even the most curious investors feeling uncertain about how to move forward with confidence. This chapter will guide you through the key rules and responsibilities connected to crypto investing. You will learn how to navigate this complex landscape, protect your profits, stay compliant with the law, and avoid common mistakes along the way.

Crypto Taxation Essentials and Smart Tracking

For most beginners, the word "tax" can make cryptocurrency feel intimidating. Crypto might look and work like digital cash, but most countries treat it differently when it comes to taxes. Governments see cryptocurrencies as "property" or digital assets, not as money. This means selling, swapping, or even spending your coins can create something called a taxable event. Simply holding your crypto is not taxed; only certain actions trigger taxes.

Think of crypto like a valuable comic book or a rare sneaker. If you buy a sneaker and keep it on your shelf, there's no tax. If you sell it later for more than you paid, you might owe tax on the profit. With crypto, taxable events usually include:

- Selling coins for cash (like turning Bitcoin into dollars)
- Trading one crypto for another (such as swapping Ethereum for Solana)
- Using crypto to buy something (for example, paying for coffee with Dogecoin)
- Getting paid in crypto for work or earning coins from mining

Whenever one of these events happens, you may owe taxes based on how much your coins changed in value. This is where "capital gains" come into play. "Capital gains" just means the profit you make when you sell or trade something for more than you paid for it. If you bought Bitcoin at $10,000 and sold it at $20,000, the $10,000 profit counts as a capital gain, which may be taxed.

Here's another term you'll see: "cost basis." "Cost basis" means the original amount you spent on your crypto, including any fees. If you bought 1 Bitcoin for $10,000, that's your cost basis. When you sell that Bitcoin, the difference between your cost basis and the selling price is your gain or loss. It works almost like keeping score in a game; what you started with versus what you ended up with tells you if you won or lost.

Taxable events do not happen when you buy crypto with regular money and just let it sit in your wallet. Nothing happens tax-wise until you sell, swap, or spend your coins. If you are rewarded with crypto, such as getting paid for a job, earning some from a staking program, or mining new coins, these are usually counted as regular income, just like if your job paid you in dollars.

Basic Record-Keeping for Crypto Taxes

To keep things stress-free, build the habit of documenting every transaction. Accurate records make everything easier, both for reporting taxes and for keeping track of your profits and losses. You only need a few details for each trade or transfer:

- The date of the transaction
- The type and amount of cryptocurrency (e.g., 0.2 Bitcoin)
- The value in local currency at the time
- What happened (e.g., sold Bitcoin for cash, traded Ethereum for Litecoin)
- Any fees paid

You can start with a simple spreadsheet. Here is a basic layout: "Capital gains" helps eliminate the "Where did I buy that?" panic at tax time. Taking a minute to add a new row after every crypto move will save you many headaches later. If remembering is hard, set a phone reminder to update your log once a week.

Helpful Tools for Tracking Transactions

Manual tracking works, but specialized tools can make life simpler. Popular tax-tracking apps and platforms such as Koinly, CoinTracker, and CryptoTaxCalculator are used by many beginners and seasoned investors alike.

These apps connect to your wallets and exchanges and automatically pull in your purchases, sales, swaps, and income. Most provide real-time dashboards that show what your portfolio is worth and label each transaction. When tax season rolls around, many can generate downloadable summaries or starter tax forms, which you or your accountant can use directly.

It feels overwhelming at first, but these tools break everything down into clear categories and numbers. You'll see all your crypto activity in one place. This not only lowers stress but also helps you catch errors, like a missed trade or a deposit you forgot to log. Despite the small fees associated with these services, many beginners find the peace of mind they provide to be worth it.

Staying Calm and Building Good Habits

Most people worry about taxes when it's already time to file, which can create anxiety. The best way to avoid feeling swamped is to work in small batches all year long. You don't need to be perfect; just write down every trade and check your logs monthly. Use break reminders to prompt yourself. If you fall behind, update your records as soon as possible and do not let confusion grow.

Governments use tax laws to bring some order and predictability to the new world of digital assets. Tax rules don't just collect revenue; they protect honest investors as well. How do regulators make sure crypto stays fair and safe? Why are rules needed in a world built on freedom and innovation? These are questions every investor will start to see as their journey continues.

Navigating Government Regulation and Staying Compliant

Imagine moving coins from one country to another, only to discover that local rules have changed overnight. Around the world, governments are developing new ways to monitor, control, or even encourage cryptocurrency adoption. For investors, understanding these rules isn't just about filing tax forms; every action, from trading to holding tokens, can depend on how local authorities see crypto. Take the United States: the government treats crypto as property, and new laws sometimes target exchanges with tougher identity checks or require all transactions above a certain value to be disclosed. Meanwhile, in El Salvador, Bitcoin is the official currency, meaning people can use it for payments anywhere. On the other side, China regularly steps in to limit trading, ban mining, or order exchange closures, making direct participation for ordinary people much harder.

Europe stands between these approaches. The European Union wants each member country to set basic crypto rules while working toward region-wide standards. In places like Germany and Switzerland, investors find stronger protections and clear legal paths, provided they use regulated exchanges and stick to the rules. Many Asian countries, like Japan and South Korea, follow similar models, tightly licensing platforms but still supporting active trading. These contrasts matter for investors because local laws determine what wallets you can use, which exchanges allow you to open an account, and whether profits are legal to bring home. Even if you live in a country with loose oversight, using a popular global exchange could bring you under much stricter rules set by the exchange's home country.

Consider what happens when rules shift quickly. A government may suddenly demand that all users verify their identities before withdrawing funds. Some investors, unable or unwilling to provide documents, may lose access to their holdings for weeks or longer. In another situation, a regulator could demand that exchanges in their region delist certain tokens or stop doing business with other countries. This can disrupt trading, freeze assets, or force coins into complicated withdrawal processes that carry added risk or cost.

Common regulatory events often shake up investors with little warning. A country might ban anonymous wallets overnight, sending panic through the markets as people scramble to secure or transfer their coins. Unlicensed exchanges can shut down unexpectedly if found breaking rules, leaving customers scrambling to retrieve their funds. These situations reveal why most governments develop regulations: to limit scams, stop money laundering, trace criminal actions, or protect newcomers from getting burned by fraudulent offers.

Keeping compliant and safe means developing a few simple habits. Before sending funds or buying coins, always check an exchange's registration status. Legitimate platforms mention their approvals in public areas, like the front page or in their user agreements. Set a routine to scan for announcements in your exchange's news section or social media accounts. These updates often warn of policy changes, new verification needs, or deadlines for users to update their profiles.

Legal Best Practices for Everyday Investors

1. Read and save the user agreement or compliance section from any platform you use.
2. Complete all requested "Know Your Customer" steps when prompted; uploading identity documents is now a standard process for most reputable exchanges.
3. Use only wallets and platforms that are registered or clearly regulated in your country or region.
4. Subscribe to official regulatory alerts or industry newsletters to spot new laws or scams.
5. Regularly review your exchange accounts for compliance notices, and make sure your account details are current.
6. Make a habit of moving funds only when you're confident the transaction won't break local laws. When in doubt, seek guidance from a trusted professional or legal advisor.

Stay sharp when presented with "too good to be true" investment offers. These often come from platforms with no physical address, no named management, or vague company details. Red flags also include exchanges that never ask for identification or force you to move funds via untraceable methods. When uncertain, stick with well-known brands that remain transparent about their headquarters, registration, and company owners.

Linking regulatory awareness to profit protection is straightforward. If an investor misses a new rule or deadline, funds may stay locked in limbo during a regulatory crackdown. Acting quickly when governments raise the bar, such as by finishing new verification steps or auditing which tokens are legal to trade, can mean the difference between having usable assets and joining a line of customers waiting for their coins. Smart investors treat regulation as part of everyday portfolio management, not just as a yearly tax exercise or rare emergency step. This approach builds a habit of checking compliance as naturally as tracking prices, making profits last, and avoiding risks that turn potential gains into costly lessons.

Now that you understand how taxes and regulations shape the world of crypto investing, you're better equipped to navigate this exciting but complex space with confidence. By keeping clear records, using helpful tracking tools, and staying alert to changing rules, you can protect your profits and avoid costly mistakes. Remember, smart investing isn't just about choosing the right coins. It's also about following the laws and building habits that keep you compliant and secure. With these foundations in place, you're ready to move forward on your crypto journey, making informed decisions that help your investments grow safely and sustainably.

CHAPTER 11
WHERE CRYPTO IS HEADED NEXT

Have you ever wondered what the future holds for cryptocurrency and digital assets? With so many new terms, technologies, and trends emerging, it's easy to feel overwhelmed or unsure about where to focus your attention. How can you tell which developments are meaningful and which are just passing hype? What should you look for to invest wisely and avoid common pitfalls? These questions are becoming more important as crypto moves beyond niche communities into mainstream finance and everyday life.

This chapter will explore the key movements shaping crypto's future and offer practical ways to stay informed and make smart decisions. You'll learn about the forces driving change in digital ownership, virtual worlds, and institutional involvement. We'll also cover how to find reliable information, evaluate new projects carefully, and build habits that help you navigate this fast-changing landscape with confidence. Whether you're entirely new or just cautious about jumping in, this guide aims to give you clear steps toward understanding and participating in the next phase of cryptocurrency.

Emerging Trends and Future Technologies in Crypto

Everyday life is becoming more connected to digital assets, shifting the way value, identity, and opportunity flow through technology. At the core of this shift are three forces. Web3 brings new ways to own and control online identity, the metaverse turns digital activity into true experience and property, and institutional investment signals that crypto is not just hype but a maturing part of the economy. Even people brand new to cryptocurrency will feel the changes brought by these trends.

Web3 stands for a new version of the internet built on blockchains. Unlike earlier platforms where big companies hold your data and accounts, Web3 spreads control out across networks, giving power back to individual users. Imagine logging into a website or app, not with a standard username, but by connecting a digital wallet that stores your unique identity and assets. No company can take it away, freeze it, or use your details for hidden profit. If you buy a song or game item as an NFT, you actually own it. You can sell, lend, or gift it without risking deletion when a company shuts down. For young professionals, this can mean controlling your professional reputation or creative work, for investors it opens the door to new types of ownership, no longer bound by the rules of banks or large tech platforms.

Layered into this vision is the rise of the metaverse, a network of virtual worlds where people work, play, and do business with real stakes. Instead of just browsing the web or checking an app, users can meet in 3D spaces, own land, or operate businesses using digital currency. Leading companies and small developers alike are pouring energy into these new experiences. Crypto and NFTs tie directly to these digital worlds. Picture buying a wearable outfit for your avatar, securing a virtual desk job in an office that pays in cryptocurrency, or attending a live concert where tickets are blockchain-verified to prevent scams. These are not sci-fi fantasies. Already, fashion labels sell virtual clothes, real estate changes hands inside games, and social lives blend with crypto-powered communities. For anyone weary of traditional work or searching for new markets, the metaverse blurs the line between play and profit.

Not everything in crypto relies on buzz or fringe communities. Some of the world's largest banks, funds, and payment outlets now create real-world gateways into digital assets. When long-standing names start buying and holding cryptocurrencies, launching trading services, or building related products, it marks a shift from decentralized hobbyists to mainstream finance. Take a look at recent headlines: Payment companies add the option to buy crypto alongside dollars. Hedge funds and retirement groups allocate a slice of holdings to Bitcoin or Ethereum, treating them with the same seriousness as stocks. This growing interest doesn't just bring new money. It steers the industry toward greater security rules and risk checks while also building trust among cautious first-time buyers. The change is driving more stable prices, better safeguards, and reliable practices, all signals that the wild-west days of crypto are giving way to a more grounded, widely accepted system.

Ethereum, as one of the key platforms at the heart of these changes, offers a striking example of technical evolution. Most early cryptocurrencies, including Bitcoin, use what's called proof-of-work. This means powerful computers have to solve difficult puzzles to add records to the blockchain, burning lots of energy and favoring those with expensive machines. Ethereum has started switching to proof-of-stake. Under this system, anyone with coins can help run the network just by "staking" them, a bit like leaving cash in a secure box to support the system, and receive rewards in return. There is no need for special gear or sky-high electricity bills. More people can join in, reducing barriers and saving energy. For instance, a college student with $500 worth of Ethereum can stake it and earn small returns, while a large investor can do the same with much larger sums.

On top of this, Ethereum keeps rolling out updates that target speed, cost, and how many transactions can run at once. Recent improvements aim to lower fees when using decentralized apps, expand the types of deals that smart contracts can handle, and lessen technical roadblocks for both users and creators. These upgrades make it easier to launch new DeFi apps for borrowing, lending, or insuring assets, as well as supporting creative uses like digital art and music NFTs.

All these forces, including decentralized control with Web3, creative experiences in the metaverse, trusted financial backing from major institutions, and the technological advances of Ethereum, work together to drive progress. They increase adoption, create new ways for people to participate, and help reduce some of the older risks.

At the same time, important questions remain. Can these developments make crypto safer for everyone, or will new risks emerge? How will regulations keep up, and what happens when large financial players interact with small online communities?

Whether you are new to crypto or have been involved for years, staying informed and adaptable is essential. The pace of change guarantees both surprises and opportunities in the road ahead.

Staying Informed and Navigating Crypto's Rapid Change Responsibly

Stepping from the latest headlines about Ethereum and Web3, readers soon realize that knowing where crypto is headed takes more than staying on top of a news cycle. Each new feature, protocol, or digital asset launches with excitement, and old rules shift quickly. Adapting to this pace means setting up daily habits for learning and balancing enthusiasm with care.

A solid starting point is building a list of reliable information outlets. Instead of jumping from social media rumor to rumor, turn to sources valued for transparency, research, and community feedback.

Trusted Crypto News & Analysis

- CoinDesk: latest news and opinion
- The Block: headlines and market analysis
- Decrypt: educational explainers, industry updates

Research Platforms

- Messari: in-depth project reports and analytics
- Glassnode: blockchain data, investor trends

Official Blogs

- Ethereum Foundation, Solana Foundation: direct from the protocol's teams

Different people learn in different ways, so beyond websites, explore other tools to make learning stick.

- **Newsletters:** Curated newsletters give quick daily or weekly updates. The Pomp Letter and Bankless help readers catch key trends without sifting through endless feeds.
- **Podcasts:** "Unchained" by Laura Shin and "Crypto Top Trading Signals" bring market analysis and interviews directly to your earbuds.
- **YouTube Channels:** DataDash or Coin Bureau explain trends in plain language for visual learners.

Not every valuable lesson comes from a news site or media personality. Community spaces fill knowledge gaps and let beginners ask questions with less fear of being out of place.

Online Forums and Groups:

- Reddit's r/CryptoCurrency and r/ethfinance
- Discord servers run by blockchain projects or focused on trading

Offline Opportunities:

- Local crypto meetups, seminars, or even live conferences

In community chats, real experiences and warning stories mix with fast tips about emerging scams or smart contract flaws, grounding recent headlines with firsthand insight.

As the market shifts, so do popular projects, and it is tempting to chase the next big thing. Instead, move slowly and use a structured approach to test value and reduce risk.

Four Steps for Evaluating New Projects

1. **Read the Whitepaper:** Check for clear explanations and defined problems. Is it easy to follow or full of vague promises?
2. **Research the Team:** Search for their public work, past projects, and their visibility in the industry.
3. **Analyze Utility & Tokenomics:** Identify what the token does, its distribution, and any built-in incentives or red flags like unchecked minting.
4. **Cross-Reference Experts & Community:** Look for expert opinion pieces, and see how communities discuss the project openly.

When Ethereum competitors like Solana or Cardano appeared, early investors compared testnet activity, developer engagement, and actual product use, not just announcements. NFT collectibles like CryptoPunks drew sustained interest not because they were hyped, but because of traceable ownership, visible developers, and lasting communities. These are examples of "trust but verify."

With swift information comes noise, and even experienced readers feel lost or overwhelmed. A helpful routine is to schedule a regular "learning audit." Every week, set aside time to:

- Review the top news stories that may affect your holdings.
- Check the latest project updates or white papers of assets you hold.
- Evaluate your portfolio's performance and any biases (such as holding too much of one token).
- Delete or stop following sources that cause anxiety, distractions, or seem to chase clicks over facts.

Think of this like preparing for travel. You don't book a trip based on a single ad or post. Instead, you read reviews, check official sites, ask friends, and compare prices. In crypto, each source offers part of the story. Only a full picture can guide you safely.

Exploring new tokens and platforms asks for a mix of curiosity and skepticism. Remember the many DeFi "rug pulls," where charismatic teams vanished with funds. Look out for "too good to be true" returns or coins promoted by celebrities with no track record. When emotions run high and crowds race to buy in, your strongest safeguard is to pause, verify details, and stick to a checklist.

Every reader brings different goals, timelines, and comfort levels. Write down your risk tolerance and what you hope to achieve, whether it's steady growth, supporting a cause, or funding a future purchase. Keep a "learning and investing checklist" close by with points like

- Did I research this project beyond social media?
- Am I risking more than I can lose?
- Is my decision based on evidence or fear of missing out?

This checklist will help anchor actions to a thoughtful plan and keep excitement productive, rather than reckless.

Staying ahead in crypto is not a sprint for hot tips. It's a habit of constant learning, careful filtering, structured evaluation, and honest self-reflection. This process gives any reader the confidence to participate wisely, no matter what the next headline promises.

Now that we understand the key trends and strategies shaping cryptocurrency's future, from Web3 and the metaverse to institutional involvement and evolving platforms like Ethereum, we are better equipped to navigate this fast-changing world with confidence. Embracing a habit of ongoing learning, careful research, and thoughtful evaluation will help you separate real opportunities from hype and risks. By staying informed through trusted sources, engaging with communities, and following a structured approach to investing, you can take control of your digital journey and make smarter choices. The path ahead may be full of surprises, but with clear guidance and steady curiosity, you're ready to participate wisely and turn today's innovations into tomorrow's possibilities.

CHAPTER 12
YOUR CRYPTO GAME PLAN

"Where do I even start with crypto?" It's a question many newcomers ask as they scan endless posts, tweets, and videos promising quick riches. The cryptocurrency world can seem like a confusing maze, filled with loud voices pulling you in different directions. Without a clear plan, it's easy to feel overwhelmed or make decisions based on hype and fear.

Developing a practical game plan is the key to navigating this fast-moving market with confidence. This chapter guides you through setting clear goals that match your comfort with risk and time commitment, building steady learning habits, and finding reliable sources of information. You'll also discover how to connect with supportive communities and take thoughtful action, so you can move forward without getting lost in noise or falling for scams. With a solid strategy in place, the path to smart crypto investing becomes clearer and more manageable.

Goal-Setting and Lifelong Learning Strategies

Stepping into the world of cryptocurrency can feel like standing at the edge of a maze. For beginners, it's easy to get swept up in bold promises and rapid-fire opinions that flood the internet. That's why building your own crypto game plan comes first. Before buying any coin or following the crowd. Your plan centers your decisions, helps you stay disciplined during wild price swings, and guards you from making snap judgments based on fear or excitement. Here, the focus lands on setting real goals, building learning habits, and knowing where to find honest information. This way, you keep your journey organized and grounded from day one.

People enter crypto for all sorts of reasons. Some individuals aspire to engage in trading as a means of generating rapid profits, closely monitoring the minute-by-minute movements of prices and anticipating profits during the subsequent surge. Others take a calmer approach, investing small amounts over months or years to watch them grow. Many start just to learn how digital currencies work, curious about blockchain and eager to experiment. It's common to feel pulled in several directions at once, so the first step is asking yourself, "Why am I here?"

Sit down and write what you hope to achieve. Are you hoping to save for a trip, dreaming of retirement income, or simply curious about the buzz? Think about your comfort with risk. How would you feel if your $100 shrank to $60 overnight? How much time are you willing to dedicate? Five minutes a day, or an hour each week? Be honest, and put it on paper. For example, you might write, "I plan to buy and hold $200 in Bitcoin and Ethereum for at least 12 months," or "My goal is to learn how exchanges work, so I'll make one small transaction per month." These statements keep you focused when social media is hyping the latest coin. They advise you to maintain your own pace and resist the temptation to act quickly when prices rise or fall.

Clear goals are more than just good intentions. They influence all your future decisions, from what platforms you join to what research you do. A well-defined plan cuts down on emotional trading and helps you resist the pressure to follow trends or online "gurus." It gives you permission to learn at your speed and to say "no" to risky bets that don't fit your aims.

Once you have your reason for entering crypto, the next piece is learning. On a schedule that works for you. The crypto landscape constantly changes. New coins launch, regulations shift, and scams pop up overnight. The best way to stay ahead is to form steady habits. Try dedicating 15 minutes a day to checking a trusted crypto news site, or schedule an hour on Sundays to read about a concept you don't yet grasp, such as how a wallet works or what blockchain actually means. Even short, regular sessions will help you filter out noise and spot patterns.

False claims and fake "experts" spring up everywhere. Learn how to spot red flags. If someone guarantees profits, claims to have secret knowledge, or pushes you to act urgently ("Buy now or miss out!"), pause and investigate. No one can promise gains in this market. Be careful with influencers who show off their wealth or refuse to explain their reasoning. Their goal is often attention, not your education. Social media trends can lure beginners into risky projects based on excitement, not facts.

Curiosity is your best defense against hype. Don't just trust a single source. Double-check what you read. If you see a claim that a new token will triple in value, search for details from at least two other places, such as established news sites or well-known analysts. Reliable news outlets often present both sides of a story, showing potential gains and possible drawbacks. When someone simply shouts about the "next big thing," compare it to a resource that patiently explains how the project works, its track record, and risks.

Here is how the difference might look:

- A flashy influencer on a video says, "Double your money in days with this secret coin!"
- A trusted analyst writes, "This project has potential but also serious risks, such as low trading volume and unclear leadership."

If you make decisions based on the first message, you risk losing funds on an unproven scheme. By choosing the second, you learn to weigh both positives and negatives. Use multiple sources before acting, and avoid echo chambers where only one view is allowed.

This focus on clear goal-setting, steady habits, and careful source-checking forms the strong base for moving forward. With your plan in hand and your mind attuned to quality information, the path ahead becomes more manageable. Soon, you can turn your goals into action by finding supportive communities and trustworthy resources to help you keep learning without losing your way in the noise.

Connecting, Staying Updated, and Taking Action

Cryptocurrency can feel like a noisy, confusing crowd full of big promises and urgent warnings. To make wise choices, it helps to not only rely on your skills but also tap into supportive communities and trusted resources. When someone first enters the crypto world, it's easy to lose themselves in the excitement or succumb to skepticism. A smart game plan involves surrounding yourself with reliable voices and clear information while learning how to judge the difference between solid advice and empty hype.

Finding the Right Crypto Community

Communities offer more than just tips or the latest price predictions. They can be a shield against scams and a support system for real learning. A healthy crypto community shares ideas in a respectful way. Members listen, answer beginner questions patiently, and value honesty. When someone posts a question about wallets or security, helpful replies focus on clear explanations, not just "buy now" promotions or referral links. Good communities also make their rules clear from the start, and there's always some kind of moderation to keep conversations safe. Scammers and aggressive promoters are dealt with quickly, and everyone knows that quick-rich schemes are not welcome. In a trusted space, you won't find bullying or people mocking those who make mistakes. Instead, experienced users step in to help without pushing anyone toward risky trading or coins nobody understands. Local meetups and online groups can both offer real connections, but always check how the group responds to new members before joining in fully.

Picking Trusted Crypto Resources

Quality resources help you build confidence step by step. Clear online tutorials, beginner-friendly books with positive reviews, and widely recognized education platforms stand out. When a book or website uses simple language, shows both benefits and risks, and covers topics from wallets to security, it becomes valuable over time. Be wary of flashy sites that push courses promising "guaranteed profits" or recommend coins about to "explode." Instead, look for lessons that help you think for yourself, such as analyzing blockchain explorers, reading actual whitepapers, or breaking down how a project's technology works. Official blogs and developer forums can be excellent for deep dives, but always check who is posting and whether the content is updated regularly. Resources that gloss over the difficult aspects or concentrate primarily on persuading you to purchase their own product should cause concern. The best resources show you how to check facts for yourself, so you're less dependent on the next guru or social media "influencer."

Spotting Reliable Crypto News

Staying up to date is important, but it matters where your news comes from. A trusted crypto news outlet names its authors, shows their background, and includes links to sources and official statements. Articles focus on the facts, such as changes in regulation, adoption by companies, or security incidents, without wild predictions. You'll see transparency about advertisers and clear lines between news and opinion. If you come across a government decision that impacts cryptocurrency, it's important to consult reputable sites that provide a clear explanation, include quotes from both sides, and refrain from declaring that a crash is imminent or that prices are skyrocketing. In contrast, sites that use clickbait headlines, urge you to trade fast, or mention secret insider tips are often looking for quick clicks or have hidden sponsors. When news breaks, compare a few reliable sources rather than rushing to act on the first alert.

Avoiding Information Overload

Crypto moves fast, but you don't have to chase every update. Having too many apps or news feeds makes decision-making harder. To keep your focus, limit yourself to a handful of trusted communities and sources. Turn off alerts that aren't urgent, and set times each week when you'll check in for updates and research. Keep a personal list of your "go-to" sites and communities, so you're not tempted by strangers or random tips. Fewer, better sources mean less stress and clearer thinking.

Actionable Crypto Checklist

1. Pick one beginner-friendly crypto community and make an introduction post.
2. Bookmark two reputable crypto news sites and sign up for their weekly digests.
3. Choose an online tutorial or book that explains key crypto concepts and review one lesson per week.
4. Make a list of common red flags for scams: pushy private messages, guarantees of quick profits, unclear project details, or secret insider info.
5. Create a folder for official project links, white papers, or educational resources that you trust most.
6. Turn off non-essential notifications and schedule two sessions per week to catch up on news.
7. Practice checking the source of every major headline before reacting or sharing.

8. Share something helpful or ask a thoughtful question in your chosen community to start building positive connections.

A strong community, quality resources, and reliable news set the foundation for a calm, confident crypto journey. With a simple plan and steady habits, taking control of your learning becomes possible, letting you move forward with clarity instead of confusion.

Now that you've learned how to set clear goals, build steady learning habits, and find trustworthy communities and resources, you're ready to take confident steps in the cryptocurrency world. With a practical plan and reliable information guiding your decisions, you can avoid common pitfalls and stay focused on what matters most. By connecting with supportive groups and checking facts carefully, you'll navigate this fast-changing space with calm and clarity. Remember, success in crypto doesn't come from chasing every trend but from thoughtful action and continuous learning, so keep your goals in sight and move forward steadily toward your own version of success.

BE THE VOICE THAT GUIDES THE NEXT INVESTOR FORWARD

At the heart of life, we rise by lifting others. Every time we share our experiences, we create a **bridge for someone who is just starting out**.

Think back. How did you feel when you first heard about *cryptocurrency*? **Excited? Confused? Unsure where to begin?**

Now imagine a beginner standing at that same crossroads, overwhelmed by talk of *Bitcoin, Ethereum, NFTs,* and all the rest. They're eager to learn but don't know which resources to trust.

That's where **your review** comes in. By leaving your *honest thoughts*, you help future readers see whether this guide gave you the **clarity, confidence, and strategies** they're looking for.

Your words can have a **ripple effect**. Making sure another curious beginner doesn't give up too soon but instead takes their **first smart step into crypto investing**.

Thank you so much for reading, learning, and now *considering sharing your voice*. Together, we can make the world of cryptocurrency more approachable, **one review at a time**.

CONCLUSION

You've reached the final page of this book, but your journey into the world of cryptocurrency is just beginning. If you made it here, chances are you're still a little curious, maybe even excited, and perhaps, like most people at this stage, a bit cautious. That's wonderful. In crypto, curiosity drives discovery, and caution keeps your savings safe. No matter what you've read elsewhere, you don't have to be a tech wizard or financial genius to take part in this new frontier. You just need an open mind, a willingness to learn, and a plan.

Let's look back at what you've accomplished so far. You now know what Bitcoin and Ethereum are and why these digital assets matter beyond their price tags. You understand the basics of blockchain technology, not through dense jargon but in clear, practical terms. You've learned how to create your first wallet, store your private keys securely, and navigate exchanges confidently without getting lost in hype or confusing acronyms. Most importantly, you now have the tools to make your first investment wisely, balancing opportunity with risk and caution with optimism.

In a world overflowing with information, some helpful and much of it misleading, you chose to focus on clarity and simplicity. That choice matters. Many people stay on the sidelines because they believe crypto is too complicated or think that missing the early days means it's too late to start. The truth is much more encouraging: there is always room for newcomers. Every day, ordinary people who take the time to learn, ask questions, and act with intention create new possibilities.

Crypto investing isn't about chasing the wildest headlines or trying to predict the next overnight sensation. It's about understanding the fundamentals, protecting your assets, and making strategic decisions that fit your life. That's why throughout this book, we focused less on picking "the best coin" and more on giving you the confidence to choose for yourself, backed by real knowledge instead of gut feelings or online rumors.

Now, you stand at the edge of a genuine financial revolution. Digital assets are challenging long-held ideas about money, ownership, and trust. Decentralized finance (DeFi), non-fungible tokens (NFTs), and smart contracts are no longer just buzzwords; they are reshaping industries as diverse as art, music, gaming, and banking. Even if you only begin with a small investment, you are part of something much larger than yourself. This space is still young, and everyone, including experts, is learning as they go. That makes it exciting, but it also leaves room for mistakes. Staying grounded in research and skepticism, rather than acting out of fear of missing out, is your greatest strength.

If you remember one lesson from these pages, let it be this: crypto is not an all-or-nothing gamble. You are free to start small, no matter what trends or influencers suggest. Your security comes from understanding the basics well, from double-checking wallet addresses before transfers, keeping seed phrases offline, and never sharing private keys, to using strong passwords and enabling two-factor authentication. These small habits, practiced consistently, will protect your assets far better than any promise of instant riches.

But safety doesn't mean staying on the sidelines forever. Most experienced investors began with a single step - their first Bitcoin, a fraction of Ethereum, or a carefully chosen altcoin. Risks exist, but so do opportunities. By reading this book, you've already set yourself apart from many who jump in blindly or give up too soon. You now have a clear foundation for thoughtful, confident action. here to stay

Remember, markets rise and fall, but the transformative potential of blockchain technology is. Some coins will disappear, others will thrive, and new innovations will continue to emerge. That's part of what makes this field both challenging and rewarding. The people who benefit most are those who combine curiosity with caution and boldness with preparation, qualities you've strengthened throughout this learning journey.

Keep reaching for reliable sources, join trustworthy communities, ask clear questions, and share what you learn. Every year, new scams and get-rich-quick schemes appear, but better tools for research and protection also emerge. Staying informed is a lifelong process, not a one-time task. Don't be afraid to adjust your strategies as the landscape evolves. That's what the best investors do. Success in crypto, as in anything else, comes from steady growth, not shortcuts.

Let's talk about what happens next. Maybe you feel ready to buy your first coin, or perhaps you want to practice setting up wallets and trying out small transactions. Wherever you are, start simple. Choose one reputable exchange, one secure wallet, and one clear goal for your first purchase, whether it's holding long-term, experimenting with DeFi, or learning how transfers work. Write down your reasons, track your experiences, and review them regularly. These early steps will teach you more than any article or influencer ever could.

If you hit a roadblock or worry that you've made a mistake, remember that everyone was a beginner once. The most successful crypto investors aren't the ones who picked the right coin first; they're the ones who kept learning, adapted when necessary, and stayed patient during uncertain times. Progress may feel slow, but every small step builds confidence and knowledge. The fact that you've taken the time to educate yourself already places you ahead of most people.

Looking forward, the future of crypto is unwritten. Challenges will come, but so will opportunities for creativity, freedom, and growth that traditional finance could never offer. Whether your goal is long-term wealth building, portfolio diversification, supporting innovation, or simply becoming more financially aware, you already have the tools to begin.

So here's your first real challenge: don't wait until you feel completely ready. Start with one carefully chosen coin, one secure wallet, and one clear goal. Take a deep breath, double-check your steps, and take action today. The new financial frontier rewards those who are prepared, not those who wait for perfection. The most important thing is to begin.

This is your invitation to join a movement that's transforming how the world views money and value. None of us knows exactly what the next decade will bring, but we do know it will reward the curious, the cautious, and the courageous. The path ahead is yours to explore. Welcome to the new financial frontier.

PART TWO
CRYPTOCURRENCY INVESTING 101

CRYPTOCURRENCY INVESTING 101: DISCOVER THE MOST LUCRATIVE WAYS TO PROFIT WITH CRYPTO, BITCOIN, ETHEREUM, ALTCOINS, NFTS, AND BLOCKCHAIN—MASTER THE ART OF WEALTH WITHOUT LIMITS

INTRODUCTION

Imagine waking up one morning and discovering that the financial world has fundamentally changed, with new rules, new players, and entirely new ways to create wealth. In many ways, that is precisely what is happening right now. We are experiencing a digital financial revolution in which cryptocurrencies and blockchain technology are transforming not only our understanding of money but also the ability for anyone, anywhere, to build genuine wealth from the ground up.

If you are holding this book, chances are you have already felt the tremors of this shift. Maybe it was a friend who suddenly started talking about Bitcoin at dinner, or a news story highlighting astonishing gains and equally shocking losses. Perhaps you have even experimented with cryptocurrency, buying a few coins through an app and watching the prices rise and fall. Whether you are simply curious or cautiously optimistic, there is a good reason why you, and millions of others, are asking: Can I actually profit from crypto? And if so, what is the smartest way to do it?

Let us be clear. Crypto is no longer just a buzzword for tech enthusiasts or a playground for risk-takers. It is becoming the new frontier of modern wealth building, one filled with both opportunity and risk, much like the gold rush or the early days of Wall Street.

Yet for every genuine chance to succeed in this space, there is also hype, misinformation, and the occasional scam. The headlines often make it seem as though everyone is either getting rich overnight or losing everything they own. The truth lies somewhere in between, and it rewards those who approach this world with clear eyes and a thoughtful plan.

This book exists to show that navigating the crypto landscape does not have to be confusing, overly technical, or limited to insiders. It is written for ambitious people who want to learn, not just watch from the sidelines, as this new asset class evolves. You might be a professional looking to diversify beyond stocks and real estate, a freelancer aiming to grow your savings, or an entrepreneur seeking financial freedom on your own terms. Maybe you follow finance channels, read newsletters, or listen to podcasts in search of your next opportunity. What unites readers like you is a willingness to take action, a tolerance for calculated risk, and a desire to understand the forces shaping our financial future rather than simply chasing them.

The first myth I want to dispel is the belief that crypto is a passing fad, destined for oblivion like dot-com penny stocks or Beanie Babies. In reality, the technology behind cryptocurrencies, known as blockchain, has already rewritten the rules of ownership, trust, and value exchange around the world. More importantly, the growth of crypto assets is being driven not by speculation alone but by genuine innovation. Entire sectors of the economy are being reimagined. From decentralized finance (DeFi) protocols that eliminate middlemen, to non-fungible tokens (NFTs) that open new markets in art and entertainment, to stablecoins that challenge the dominance of national currencies, crypto is reshaping the financial landscape in real time.

At the same time, it is important to be honest. Alongside extraordinary stories of everyday people earning life-changing profits, there are also accounts of devastating losses. The volatility can be intimidating, the jargon confusing, and the sheer number of options overwhelming. There is a steep learning curve, yet it remains one of the most dynamic and potentially rewarding areas to explore as an investor today. The difference between those who succeed and those who struggle is not insider information or advanced technical knowledge. It comes down to having a clear, actionable plan and the willingness to learn, adapt, and make informed decisions.

That is exactly what this book aims to deliver. In the chapters ahead, you will move beyond the noise and the memes to gain a solid understanding of how crypto works, why it matters, and, most importantly, how to participate wisely in this evolving market. You will discover what makes assets such as Bitcoin, Ethereum, and other altcoins unique, and learn how to evaluate which projects are worth your attention and investment. We will explore multiple approaches for generating income, from simple buy-and-hold strategies to trading techniques and emerging opportunities in staking, DeFi, and NFTs. Each method carries its own risks and rewards. By the end, you will have the knowledge and confidence to build a portfolio tailored to your goals, whether you seek short-term gains or long-term generational wealth.

Crypto investing is not about chasing moonshots or falling for hype. It is about stacking small, smart decisions that add up over time. If you are reading this, you are likely not afraid of a little risk, but you are also wise enough to demand clarity before making a move. That is why I promise no fluff, no empty claims, and no vague advice. You will find only strategies and insights that help you profit from crypto, explained in plain language, supported by real examples, and grounded in realistic expectations. Every chapter is designed to give you practical steps you can apply immediately, whether you have one hundred or one hundred thousand dollars to invest.

We will start simple and build from there, making sure each concept makes sense before moving forward. You do not need to be a programmer, a math expert, or a full-time trader. All you need is curiosity, ambition, and the willingness to learn. Together we will break down complex topics into clear, manageable lessons using relatable examples and straightforward guidance. When technical terms appear, you will find explanations that go beyond definitions, giving you context so you understand why something matters and how it affects your results.

It is worth emphasizing that the stakes are real, and so are the opportunities. As banks, governments, and corporations race to adapt to rapid technological change, early adopters who educate themselves and act strategically have a rare chance to get ahead. However, crypto is not a get-rich-quick scheme, and luck alone rarely leads to lasting success. If you are hoping for a hidden shortcut, this is not that kind of book. What you will gain instead is a solid foundation, built on the same mindset and tools used by successful investors who endure both bull and bear markets, capitalize on trends, and steadily grow wealth across different cycles.

By the end of this journey, you will know how to analyze coins, recognize potential scams, and evaluate projects based on real value rather than hype. You will understand how to use wallets and exchanges safely, manage risk with confidence, and create a personalized investment plan that matches your timeline and risk tolerance. Whether your goal is to supplement your income, save for the future, or achieve financial independence from traditional systems, you will finish this book ready to make smarter, more confident choices in the fast-changing world of crypto.

The digital frontier of wealth is wide open, and the barriers to entry have never been lower. The only true limit is your willingness to learn and take action. If you are ready to move beyond fear and confusion, to cut through the noise, and to see how ordinary people are using crypto to build extraordinary opportunities, then this book is for you. Let us step forward into the future of finance together, with clarity and purpose.

CHAPTER 13
CRYPTO 101 – WHAT IT IS AND WHY IT MATTERS

What if everything you thought you knew about money was already outdated? What if the systems we have trusted for decades, including banks, governments, and financial institutions, were no longer the only way to manage, move, or grow your wealth? Imagine a world where you can send funds anywhere in minutes, without needing anyone's permission or interference. This is not a distant vision of the future. It is happening right now, and it is transforming how people across the globe think about money, power, and access.

For many, cryptocurrency still feels like a puzzle filled with technical terms and confusing hype. Yet beneath all that noise lies a simple, powerful idea that can redefine financial freedom and opportunity. The shift from traditional finance to digital currencies challenges long-standing rules and opens the door to new ways of investing, saving, and taking control of your financial life. Whether you are curious, cautious, or ready to dive in, understanding this change is the first step toward making smart and confident choices about your future.

Comparing Cryptocurrency with Traditional Finance and Foundational Concepts

The traditional financial world centers around trusted middlemen banks, governments, stock exchanges who manage the flow of money, approve transactions, and make the rules. When someone deposits their salary in a bank, the bank holds those funds, tracks their account, and verifies their money is legitimate. If they want to send money overseas, a network of banks, payment processors, and sometimes governments get involved. These layers mean international transfers can take days, come with heavy fees, and be subject to approval or delays. Account access remains at the bank's discretion, with the possibility of restrictions, freezes, or reversals if the institution suspects trouble.

Cryptocurrency rewrites these rules. Digital coins like Bitcoin and Ethereum use technology to offer direct control over funds, sidestepping the need for central managers. With crypto, sending value to someone anywhere in the world happens on a shared digital network without bank approval. Transactions can settle in minutes even across continents, often for much lower fees, regardless of local banking hours or government borders. The keys to your crypto wallet put control back in your hands, instead of letting a distant institution decide what you can or cannot do with your money.

Traditional finance stores value in physical banks or records in electronic ledgers managed by each institution. Payments and investments route through trusted third parties that can introduce cost, delay, and risk. Crypto value, in contrast, lives on a shared public blockchain. No single entity owns or controls this ledger; every participant can see and verify transactions for themselves. This structure not only changes how people move and store money but also who gets to participate. Opening a crypto wallet requires no paperwork or approval; anyone with an internet connection can use it.

Core Principles Shaping Crypto

Decentralization

The most important shift crypto offers is decentralization. Power, once consolidated in banks or central authorities, is distributed over countless computers known as nodes. Each node keeps a copy of the blockchain and validates new transactions independently. Unlike a bank, which can shut down access if a branch experiences an outage, a decentralized network stays running even if parts of it go offline. In the case of Bitcoin, people around the world maintain the same transaction database, so the service doesn't depend on a single organization or location.

Transparency

Blockchains act as public ledgers, digital books open for anyone to inspect. Every transaction ever made on a network like Ethereum or Bitcoin is visible to all users. If someone wants to check where their funds have moved or confirm the legitimacy of an address, the public record is available at any time. This transparency gives crypto a built-in self-audit feature. It fosters trust, reduces the room for manipulation, and discourages shady behavior. In traditional finance, auditing account histories can require costly legal action or negotiation with banks that may refuse to share data. In crypto, users are empowered to inspect and verify anything they want freely.

Financial Sovereignty

Crypto hands over the reins to the individual, offering full control over assets. Only the owner of private keys can move the coins in their digital wallet; no manager, clerk, or intermediary can interfere. Consider an example: someone living in one country who wants to send money home to parents abroad. Using a bank wire, the process may involve multiple checks, approvals, and steep international fees. With crypto, sending funds means authorizing a transaction from wallet to wallet. The money arrives in minutes, and no third party can freeze or block it. This level of access isn't possible with regular checking accounts, which are vulnerable to institutional controls.

How Blockchain Transforms the Economy

At the core of every cryptocurrency is blockchain technology. Imagine a digital notebook shared with everyone, where each page contains a group of transactions. Once a page is filled, it is locked in and linked forever to the next, creating a chain. Anyone can flip through these pages and review transaction details, ensuring nothing gets altered or erased. This design makes fraud very hard and guarantees a full history of what happened and when.

Blockchains let people trade, lend, and store value directly. Peer-to-peer transactions cut out middlemen such as payment processors or notaries, making deals quicker and cheaper. Businesses have started to use blockchain to track goods through supply chains knowing if a bottle of olive oil really comes from Italy, for example, or if a diamond was sourced ethically. Companies can prove the origin and journey of their products to consumers using blockchain entries.

In finance, decentralized applications replace what banks once did. People can borrow, lend, earn interest, or insure assets through code-based contracts open for anyone to see and use. Some use blockchains for digital collectibles and art known as NFTs which provide ownership records that can't be copied or faked. The impact stretches beyond banking, shaking up every line of business that used to depend on trusted third parties.

These changes open doors. Individuals can join global markets, invest, and own assets without seeking approval from big institutions. Each of these features unlocks new opportunities for people to manage, grow, and protect their wealth in ways once reserved for industry insiders. As readers take in these distinctions and principles, it becomes clear how the world of crypto invites a fresh, more direct approach to building financial independence and exploring the future of investing.

Crypto's Disruptive Nature and Personal Relevance

Decentralization stands at the heart of the disruption caused by cryptocurrency in the world of finance. In traditional systems, transactions must be approved by banks or credit unions, which act as powerful middlemen. Imagine needing a banker's sign-off just to send money to a friend in another country, then waiting several days with fees deducted at every step. With crypto, individuals send value directly to anyone on the globe almost instantly, with no approval or bank gatekeeping required. This feature alone introduces a new sense of freedom, like being able to write and mail your letter anywhere in the world without relying on a postal worker to read or stamp it first. The blockchain, a digital ledger that records every transaction publicly, replaces centralized oversight with transparency everyone can trust.

In this way, cryptocurrencies like Bitcoin or Ethereum challenge long-standing structures by removing gatekeepers and giving power back to users. The rules of the network are enforced by software, not by humans behind a counter. The implications reach further than faster payments; they allow people who have never had access to formal banking to transact, save, and invest with just an internet connection. Crypto does not care about citizenship, employment history, or the status of your local economy. If you have a smartphone or computer, you can set up a free wallet, buy or receive tiny amounts of any coin, and become a participant.

Traditional investing often comes with barriers: high minimum deposits, lengthy approval processes, and requirements to pass credit or identification checks. Crypto's entry points are much easier to access. You do not need to "qualify" to open a wallet, nor do you need permission to participate in a decentralized finance (DeFi) protocol. With DeFi tools, regular people access peer-to-peer lending, borrowing, and earning interest by supplying funds directly into liquidity pools. Many services let users buy fractions of coins, making it possible to start with even a few dollars. There are platforms where you can stake coins to support the network and earn rewards, or pool your money with others to maximize returns. These opportunities appear instantly on your screen, without negotiation with a broker or bank manager.

Accessibility does not stop at low entry thresholds. The cryptocurrency market operates continuously, with prices fluctuating and traders engaging in transactions around the clock, every day of the year. There are no "market closed" notices or downtime for holidays. This setup fits those who want to invest or manage assets on their own schedule, or those across time zones who can't always work within the restrictions of traditional trading hours. Crypto treats users equally, whether they come from a major economic hub or a small, remote village.

Several practical reasons make crypto worth a spot in an investor's future plans. One, crypto gives a real way to diversify your portfolio. Its price moves are often uncorrelated with the swings in stocks or bonds. For instance, during some global downturns, while traditional markets faltered, Bitcoin not only held value but sometimes climbed. By including crypto, an investor may reduce overall risk and build a portfolio that can weather situations where other assets struggle.

Another draw lies in the variety of possible income streams. Beyond simple "buy and hold" tactics, crypto lets users put assets to work. Staking, often on networks like Ethereum or Solana, allows you to lock up coins to help validate transactions while earning returns. DeFi applications allow for lending out your crypto or providing liquidity to trading pairs, earning interest or a share of transaction fees. Even the world of NFTs (non-fungible tokens) offers artists and creators the possibility of collecting royalties every time their digital work changes hands. These options mean that earning with crypto is active, not just dependent on future price swings.

Direct asset control is another powerful motivator. With crypto, you can hold your funds without relying on a bank or investment company. Only you hold the private keys to your digital wallet, and only you decide when and how to move your assets. There are no account freezes because of third-party suspicion or arbitrary withdrawal limits. For people in places where financial surveillance is strict or capital controls are routine, this kind of autonomy offers more than convenience; it can protect savings and personal freedom.

Those who join early in a changing landscape often catch new opportunities before the world catches up. Crypto is still a young market, full of innovation. Today's users can be the first to benefit from new digital assets, automated contracts that run themselves (smart contracts), and decentralized apps that deliver services in novel ways. Early adopters have at times seen rewards not just in price growth but also in shaping how technology is built and used.

Getting involved in crypto equips investors to spot real chances for growing wealth, tell safe tools apart from scams, and build strategies that match their own risk comfort and ambitions. By understanding these changes and possibilities, readers position themselves to act wisely and flexibly in the evolving world of finance.

Now that we understand how cryptocurrency differs from traditional finance by offering decentralization, transparency, and personal control, we can begin to see its true potential for transforming how we manage money and invest. This new financial landscape opens doors for anyone to participate in global markets with fewer barriers, faster transactions, and more ways to grow wealth through innovative tools like staking, lending, and digital collectibles. As you move forward, this foundational knowledge prepares you to build a smart, balanced crypto portfolio tailored to your goals—whether seeking steady income, diversification, or long-term growth while navigating the opportunities and challenges in this fast-evolving space. Embracing these changes means stepping into a future where financial freedom is more accessible and empowering than ever.

CHAPTER 14
THE BIG TWO – INVESTING IN BITCOIN AND ETHEREUM

Most people think of cryptocurrency as a wild and confusing frontier filled with hype and risk. In reality, among thousands of coins, two digital assets, **Bitcoin** and **Ethereum**, stand out as the foundational pillars of this new financial landscape. They are not just popular names; they represent two distinct approaches to money and technology, each with its own strengths and challenges that every investor should understand.

This chapter takes a closer look at Bitcoin and Ethereum, exploring what gives them value, how they function, and what risks they carry. You will also learn practical ways to include these core assets in your portfolio so you can find the right balance between security and growth as you build your crypto investments thoughtfully. Whether you are drawn to stability and proven value or want exposure to cutting-edge innovation, understanding these two giants will give you the clarity and confidence to move forward.

Bitcoin vs. Ethereum: Core Value, Technology, and Investment Characteristics

Bitcoin's rise started in 2009 with a single idea: create digital money that nobody could control or shut down. Satoshi Nakamoto, the anonymous creator, wrote a set of rules that all Bitcoin users follow.

A big part of this design is scarcity; there will never be more than 21 million bitcoins. Think of it like a digital version of gold: there is only so much, you can't make more, and that makes each piece more valuable if enough people want it. This capped supply stands in sharp contrast to government-issued currency, which central banks regularly print in large amounts. When currencies lose value due to inflation or economic turbulence, Bitcoin attracts people who want to protect the value of their money.

The technology behind Bitcoin is the blockchain - a public, transparent record of every movement of coins. Each transaction joins a secure chain of data shared by thousands of computers all over the world. Nobody needs to ask permission to use Bitcoin, which makes it censorship-resistant. No single government, company, or person can freeze your coins or block your payments. These qualities draw investors who fear instability or restrictions in traditional finance.

People sometimes call Bitcoin "digital gold" because, like precious metals, it acts as a store of value. Throughout history, gold has helped people hedge against inflation, government takeovers, and global shocks. Public companies like MicroStrategy and Tesla invest in Bitcoin, hoping it will outlast cash's volatility. El Salvador moved even further, adopting Bitcoin as legal tender and allowing people to use it for everyday payments alongside the U.S. dollar. Large investors and small savers alike treat Bitcoin as a secure boat in stormy economic seas.

A Bitcoin transaction works without intermediaries. When you send coins, your request is broadcast to the entire network. Miners, which are powerful computers, compete to verify and add your payment to the blockchain. This process rewards them with small amounts of newly created bitcoin, but the total supply will never exceed twenty-one million coins. Because every transaction is public and the system relies on mathematics rather than human trust or government control, long-term investors view Bitcoin as both reliable and secure.

Bitcoin's primary role is security and preservation of value, which makes it a favorite among those who prioritize stability over speculation. However, not everyone in the crypto world wants to simply hold their coins and wait for growth. This is where Ethereum enters, with a broader and more dynamic vision.

Ethereum, created by Vitalik Buterin and launched in 2015, was designed to do more than just move money. It introduced the idea of a programmable blockchain. This allows developers to write code, known as smart contracts, that lives directly on the blockchain and runs automatically without human oversight or intermediaries. The simplest way to understand a smart contract is to imagine a vending machine. You insert a coin, the machine checks the amount, and it instantly delivers the correct item—no negotiation or trust required. On Ethereum, this same logic applies to more complex actions, such as lending money, operating marketplaces, or tracking ownership of digital artwork.

Ethereum now forms the backbone of what many call the decentralized web, or Web3. Here, anyone can create and use applications that operate beyond the control of traditional companies. Examples include decentralized finance (DeFi) platforms, where people lend and borrow money using only code, with no banks involved. Decentralized exchanges like Uniswap allow users to trade cryptocurrency directly with one another at any time of day. Ethereum also opened the door to NFTs, or non-fungible tokens, which represent digital art, collectibles, and other unique assets recorded on the blockchain. Because these ownership records cannot be changed or erased, NFTs have created entirely new markets for creativity and digital property.

Ethereum remains flexible because its community constantly upgrades and improves the network. Exciting changes such as the shift from proof-of-work to proof-of-stake make Ethereum more energy-efficient and allow investors to earn rewards by locking up coins for a period (called staking). This ability to evolve keeps Ethereum at the front of blockchain innovations.

Comparing Bitcoin to Ethereum shows two powerful but different anchors in crypto. Bitcoin stands as the secure, predictable store of value, more like a digital safe than a playground for invention. Its main risks involve regulatory changes, price swings, and rare software upgrades. For example, sudden government bans or harsh regulations can cause Bitcoin's price to drop sharply, but many times it recovers as broader acceptance returns.

Ethereum carries more risk but more room for growth. Changes to the protocol, such as past hard forks or the move to staking, can push prices up or down quickly. Regulatory uncertainty affects its DeFi and NFT applications. Yet projects running on Ethereum can grow rapidly; DeFi alone grew from almost nothing to billions of dollars in assets in just a couple of years.

Understanding the differences between Bitcoin and Ethereum helps you answer a simple question: what do you expect and want from crypto? Some will use Bitcoin's safety to guard against inflation. Others will put their energy into Ethereum's fast-growing apps. Knowing the story behind each asset helps you match your investments to your goals and leaves you ready to build a portfolio designed for both security and dynamism.

Allocating and Investing: Practical Steps for Beginners

There's a clear logic behind focusing a starter crypto portfolio on Bitcoin and Ethereum, but the true challenge lies in deciding how these two assets fit your personal investment picture. Your split between Bitcoin and Ethereum depends on your goals and comfort as much as on each coin's qualities.

Step 1: Know Your Goals and Risk Preferences

Before picking numbers, it helps to pause and think about what you want from your crypto investments. Are you looking to grow your wealth over a decade, or are you hoping for quicker gains? Does steady growth mean more to you than big upside potential, even if it means missing out on sudden highs? Everyone comes to crypto with their own priorities, and these will shape how you allocate.

Real-World Scenarios

- If your main focus is preserving value over the long run, perhaps you're building for retirement or just want an asset less likely to suddenly swing; tilting toward Bitcoin can offer peace of mind. Bitcoin's track record and simple use case as "digital gold" might appeal more to those with lower risk tolerance.
- If you're younger, curious, and excited by technology and growth, and you're okay with more ups and downs along the way, you may want to give Ethereum a bigger role. Its wide range of uses and faster pace of development can lead to greater returns, but also bigger drops.
- Sometimes, you simply want a steady, no-frills split for broad exposure. In this case, a basic blend can work for nearly anybody.

Step 2: Model Your Portfolio - Concrete Allocations

To make these decisions practical and not just abstract, here are three sample allocations. These fit different types of investors and show how the balance shapes your experience.

- **Conservative Allocation (70% BTC, 30% ETH):**

  For cautious investors who want most of their crypto dollars in what's often called the steadier coin. Imagine putting $1,000 total into crypto: you'd allocate $700 to Bitcoin and $300 to Ethereum. This setup aims to cushion big swings, making it easier to sleep at night.

- **Balanced Allocation (50% BTC, 50% ETH):**

  Equal exposure to both. You get the benefits of Bitcoin's staying power and Ethereum's rapid ecosystem growth. If you want to future-proof your bet, this split gives you a foot in each world. With $2,000, you'd put $1,000 in each.

- **Growth-Focused Allocation (30% BTC, 70% ETH):**

  This strategy is ideal for investors who are chasing higher possible returns and are comfortable facing bigger price swings. Say you're investing $3,000: that makes $900 for Bitcoin and $2,100 for Ethereum. While this strategy invites more risk, it also offers a shot at stronger overall growth if Ethereum outpaces Bitcoin over time.

No split is better for everyone. These models are starting points. You can adjust for your needs. For example, if sudden losses make you anxious, stick closer to the first example. If you have a long time horizon, you can experiment with the latter.

Step 3: Start Investing; Simple First Steps

Turning plans into action is where theory meets reality. It's best to make that first investment experience as smooth and secure as possible.

1. **Open an Account on a Reputable Exchange:**

Choose a well-established exchange that supports both Bitcoin and Ethereum. Popular choices include Coinbase, Kraken, and Gemini. Set up your account, submitting verification details where required.

2. **Fund Your Account:**

Link your bank account or debit card to deposit money. Start with an amount you're comfortable with, keeping in mind your planned allocation.

3. **Buy BTC and ETH According to Your Plan:**

Use the exchange's platform to purchase Bitcoin and Ethereum in the proportions you decided. Most places let you buy fractions, so exact amounts aren't an issue.

4. **Consider Dollar-Cost Averaging:**

Instead of buying your crypto all at once, you might prefer to buy a fixed dollar amount (like $100) each week or month. This evens out your entry price over time and avoids going all-in at a market peak.

5. **Set Up Secure Storage:**

Once purchased, move your coins to a secure digital wallet if you plan to hold them for a while. Software wallets work for small sums, while large holdings are safest in hardware wallets kept offline.

Step 4: Manage and Monitor Effectively

Creating a cryptocurrency portfolio is a continuous process. Staying organized helps avoid common mistakes.

- **Rebalancing:**

  Say Bitcoin grows faster and ends up at 80% of your holdings. Consider selling some to buy more Ethereum and return to your original target. Regularly check your mix every six or twelve months.

- **Risk Controls:**

  Never invest what you can't afford to lose. Keep a portion of savings outside crypto for emergencies.

- **Security Basics:**

  Always enable two-factor authentication, beware of phishing links, and research any wallet or exchange before trusting it with your money.

- **Ongoing Reviews:**

  As your financial goals or confidence change, it's okay to tweak allocations. Small, thoughtful adjustments pay off more than big, panicked moves.

Step by step, this kind of approach helps develop habits that build confidence while keeping your portfolio on track.

Now that we've explored the unique strengths, risks, and real-world uses of Bitcoin and Ethereum, you're equipped to make informed decisions about how these core assets can fit your personal investment goals. Whether you seek the steady security of Bitcoin's digital gold or the exciting growth potential of Ethereum's programmable ecosystem, understanding their differences empowers you to build a portfolio that balances safety with opportunity. By thoughtfully choosing your allocations, starting with small, manageable steps, and staying engaged with regular reviews, you set yourself up for a smarter, more confident journey into crypto investing. With this foundation, you're ready to take action and grow your wealth in a way that fits your needs and embraces the future of finance.

CHAPTER 15
ALTCOINS AND HIDDEN GEMS

Have you ever wondered what lies beyond Bitcoin in the vast and ever-changing world of cryptocurrency? How can you tell which projects truly have potential and which are driven by hype or hidden risks? Many investors feel both curious and cautious when it comes to altcoins, the digital currencies that promise innovation but often come with uncertainty. What makes some altcoins rise as valuable investments while others fade into obscurity or even lead to losses?

If you have experimented with crypto before but want to take a smarter, more strategic approach, you are not alone. This chapter will guide you through the many different types of altcoins, how to evaluate their real worth, and how to protect yourself from common mistakes as you explore this exciting and unpredictable part of the market.

Understanding Altcoins: Types, Categories, and Major Players

In the world of cryptocurrency, altcoins include everything beyond Bitcoin. Some people treat Ethereum as its own category because of its size and influence, but technically it is an altcoin too. Altcoins span hundreds of different digital coins and tokens, each created for a unique purpose that often goes beyond simple payments. When you hear the term "altcoin," think of a fast-moving landscape filled with ideas, communities, and businesses all competing to redefine what money, platforms, or digital ownership can be.

Altcoins can be grouped into several categories based on their main functions. Payment coins, such as Litecoin and Monero, work as forms of digital cash, focusing on fast, low-cost, and secure transfers. Platform tokens, including Ethereum and Solana, act as the fuel that powers entire ecosystems, enabling decentralized apps, smart contracts, and even the creation of new tokens. Utility tokens serve a specific function or provide access to a service rather than just transferring value. For example, Chainlink is used to deliver trusted data to smart contracts.

Stablecoins take a different approach. By linking their value to real-world currencies like the US dollar, coins such as USDC or Tether aim to offer stability during volatile market conditions. Finally, governance tokens, like UNI from Uniswap, allow holders to vote on project updates and future decisions, giving users a direct voice in how the platform evolves.

Ways Altcoins Get Grouped

Investors pay close attention to how coins are grouped because these categories directly influence both risk and opportunity. Market capitalization, or market cap, remains the classic first filter. It is calculated by multiplying a token's price by the number of coins in circulation. Some of the largest altcoins by market cap include Ethereum (ETH) and Binance Coin (BNB). Because of their size and established track records, these tend to carry lower risk than smaller or newly launched tokens.

Another key factor is technological purpose. "Layer 1" coins such as Avalanche (AVAX), Cardano (ADA), and Solana (SOL) operate their own decentralized blockchains, serving as the foundation for apps, tokens, and entire projects. "Layer 2" tokens, by contrast, are built on top of major chains like Ethereum to improve transaction speed or reduce costs.

Altcoins can also be grouped by sector to help investors identify focus areas. DeFi tokens, such as AAVE and COMP, power decentralized lending and borrowing platforms. NFT ecosystem coins, including Axie Infinity Shards (AXS) and Decentraland (MANA), support gaming, virtual worlds, and digital collectibles. Some projects bridge multiple categories, but understanding their primary sector provides context and makes it easier to evaluate their purpose.

These distinctions matter because each category carries a different balance of risk and reward. A portfolio filled with small-cap NFT coins will likely rise and fall sharply with trends, while one that includes larger "layer 1" assets or stablecoins will behave more steadily. Knowing where each altcoin fits helps investors build balanced portfolios and avoid concentrating too much risk in one type of project.

Major Altcoins and Their Innovations

Some altcoins have taken center stage through popularity or new technology. Ethereum's network introduced "smart contracts," small programs that run exactly as programmed, forming the core of DeFi and NFTs. Investors use ETH for everything from running decentralized exchanges to launching collectibles. On another front, Binance Smart Chain (BNB) cuts transaction costs and processes trades quickly, making it a favorite for low-fee users. Solana is widely known for speed and the ability to handle thousands of transactions per second. Builders often select Solana for apps needing low fees and fast updates. Cardano offers a more academic approach, basing changes on research and peer reviews, which attracts those looking for something reliable and carefully managed.

Beyond payments, altcoins spark new growth areas: decentralized finance, digital voting, blockchain gaming, and linking real data to the blockchain for smart contracts. These shifts show that investing in altcoins taps into more than just currency—it's a way to access technology trends early.

Researching Altcoins Like a Pro

Finding the gold among altcoins demands careful research and professional skepticism. Start with the project's whitepaper, which explains the technology, goals, and token distribution. A strong whitepaper should be clear and detailed, outlining the use case and how the token works. Next, check out the team. Who are the founders and developers? Do they list real names and profiles? Is there an active developer community on GitHub? Frequent code updates are a sign a project is alive and improving.

Tokenomics gives clues about supply, demand, and distribution: Is the supply fixed? How are new coins released? Does the team have a huge stash, or is ownership widely shared? Security and audits matter here. Has the project been checked by trusted third-party auditors? Have any bugs or hacks happened, and if so, how were they handled?

Explore community activity. Lively chats on Twitter, Discord, or Reddit, and clear communication from the project team, point to a vibrant ecosystem. Double-check credible industry news. A loud social media presence with little substance often means hype is running ahead of progress.

Consider an example. Suppose you're looking at a new DeFi token. The whitepaper sounds exciting, but GitHub shows barely any code updates, and the founders are anonymous. Red flag. In contrast, a project like Chainlink has open development, frequent code pushes, and major integrations. This suggests substance over hype without making a judgment call to buy.

A huge world of coins brings both fresh ideas and real dangers. With so many new tokens launching, research skills keep you ahead of hype and scams, setting you up to handle even higher-risk corners of the crypto universe.

Navigating Small-Cap Coins and Avoiding Risks

When you step beyond established altcoins, the landscape becomes far less predictable. The stakes rise quickly. In this space, small-cap coins and so-called hidden gems promise fortune while concealing plenty of traps. Early-stage tokens have turned ordinary investors into millionaires overnight. New ideas, overlooked use cases, and low entry prices often tempt bold investors eager to catch the next major trend just as it begins. These projects sometimes thrive by addressing needs that larger coins overlook. For example, one coin built to help small businesses send global payments grew from pennies to dollars in a matter of weeks after a wave of users sought cheaper transactions. Another focused on NFT ticketing found rapid adoption as artists and venues searched for new ways to earn revenue. Stories like these fuel the excitement and sense of possibility that surround emerging coins.

Not every small-cap story ends well. In fact, most do not. The same qualities that make these coins appealing—newness, niche innovation, and early-stage markets—also make them risky. For every project that succeeds, countless others fade away or vanish entirely. Small-cap coins are known for extreme price swings that go far beyond what large tokens experience. Gains of 100 percent in a week can be followed by a total collapse the next. Because trading volume is low, even one large buy or sell can send prices soaring or crashing in seconds.

The dangers extend beyond volatility. Small-cap coins often attract scams, manipulation, and quick-profit schemes. One of the most common is the pump and dump. This occurs when a person or group hypes up a low-value coin using social media, chat groups, or fake news to create buzz. As more investors rush in, prices surge and appear unstoppable. Meanwhile, the promoters quietly plan their exit. Once enough new buyers have entered, they sell their holdings all at once, sending the price into free fall. Those who arrived late are left holding coins worth a fraction of what they paid. These scams thrive because oversight is limited and it is easy to fabricate online enthusiasm.

Spotting danger before you get caught takes a watchful eye and a clear routine. Warning signs rarely appear in isolation, and a single red flag is enough reason to pause or walk away. Some of the most common indicators include:

- **Thin trading volume:** If only a few trades happen each day, it means there is little demand. In a rush, you could find yourself unable to sell at any price. For example, a new coin might show wild price movements and huge percentage gains on small trades, but trying to cash out even a modest sum crashes the price.
- **Anonymous or unverifiable team:** Projects run by people with fake names or no history should set off alarms. If you cannot find details about the founders, or if the team has no public presence, there is no reason to trust them. For instance, a "world-changing" coin surfaced with a slick website and an active Telegram but offered only cartoon avatars for team bios.
- **Vague or plagiarized whitepapers:** A whitepaper that repeats buzzwords, copies content from other projects, or never quite explains why this coin matters is a bad sign. In one case, a supposedly "innovative" coin had a whitepaper that was nearly identical to older projects—change a logo here and there, but no original thinking underneath.
- **Excessive social media hype:** If most mentions of a coin come from paid promotions, spammy influencers, or viral "pump" campaigns, there's a good chance the buzz is artificial. An example is when a Twitter account with fake followers spends days promising huge returns with no clear reason why the price should rise.

- **Misleading partnerships or endorsements:** Some projects will claim to be tied to big brands or celebrities, but closer inspection falls apart. For example, a coin claimed a deal with a major payment processor, but the processor denied any link when asked.
- **Unclear token utility:** If you can't figure out what problem the token solves—or if the use case feels forced—it's likely just a vehicle for speculation. As one coin advertised "the future of finance," its actual function was just to trade back and forth with no real-world purpose.

Moving with caution means acting on these signals. Always run background checks on anyone connected to the project. Examine a project's GitHub or similar code repository to see if development is ongoing or stale. Verify that liquidity is available by checking reputable exchanges, not just obscure platforms. Review third-party research from sources that are independent and not paid to promote. Solid skepticism is a must. If something feels off, walk away; there is no shame in safety.

Avoid FOMO at all costs. Set a personal checklist before every new investment. Step back for hours, or even days, before putting money at risk. Some investors use demo accounts or simulated trades to test if their reasoning holds up under less pressure. These habits put your future back in your hands. Every move in small-cap coins should start with one question: What am I risking, and why? Staying safe means making sure the answer is always clear.

Now that you understand the diverse world of altcoins—their types, innovations, and risks—you are better prepared to spot valuable projects and steer clear of common pitfalls. With careful research, a healthy dose of skepticism, and a clear strategy, you can confidently navigate this fast-changing market and build a crypto portfolio that balances opportunity with safety. As you move forward, remember that staying informed and patient will help you avoid hype and scams, positioning you to take advantage of the exciting growth altcoins offer while protecting your investment goals.

CHAPTER 16

NFTS – INVESTING BEYOND COINS

When Sarah first heard about NFTs, she pictured digital art hanging in an online gallery, beautiful but intangible and difficult to grasp as an investment. She wondered why anyone would pay hundreds or even thousands of dollars for something that couldn't be held, touched, or easily understood, like stocks or coins. Yet stories of people earning impressive profits through NFTs kept surfacing, often alongside warnings about scams and sudden market crashes.

Confused by the mix of hype and caution, Sarah hesitated. She wasn't alone. Many investors find themselves in the same position, curious about the potential of NFTs but wary of diving in without a clear understanding of what they are, how they hold value, and what it truly takes to invest wisely.

This chapter helps navigate that uncertainty, offering a grounded look at NFTs beyond the headlines. By the end, you'll have a clear picture of how they work, what drives their value, and whether they deserve a place in your own financial strategy.

Understanding NFTs: Definitions, Valuation, and Real-World Applications

NFTs represent digital items that exist as unique entries on a blockchain, a shared digital ledger that records who owns what. The key word, non-fungible, means that each NFT is different from every other NFT, unlike cryptocurrencies such as Bitcoin or Ethereum. For example, one Bitcoin is equal in value to another and can be exchanged without any change in worth. NFTs, on the other hand, are like trading cards or autographed sneakers. Each has its own traits, history, and story that make it one of a kind and not directly interchangeable with another.

Imagine buying a limited-edition baseball card. Only a few exist, you know exactly which one you have, and collectors may pay a premium for it. With NFTs, the same concept applies digitally and on a larger scale, but with technology that verifies who truly owns the item. When someone purchases a piece of digital art as an NFT, they gain a record of ownership stored on the blockchain. This record is public, easy to verify, and cannot be faked or erased. Owning an NFT does not always mean you own the rights to copy or sell the image itself, but it does mean you own that unique, digitally signed version. Artists can upload their work to platforms like OpenSea or Foundation, set how many editions exist, and sell them as NFTs to buyers around the world. When the sale completes, the blockchain updates with the new owner's information. If someone sells the NFT later, the blockchain tracks the transfer, so buyers never have to worry about forgeries.

The value of an NFT depends on more than just the artwork or item itself. Several factors work together to determine its worth. Rarity attracts collectors who seek something truly scarce, where only a handful of versions or perhaps just one exist. The reputation and following of the creator also play a major role. A work from Beeple, the digital artist who sold “Everydays: The First 5000 Days” at Christie’s in 2021, reached 69 million dollars because of both scarcity and the artist’s global recognition. The sale proved that

NFTs can hold immense value when creative vision and cultural impact align.

Historical significance can also influence value. Was the NFT connected to a defining moment in technology, gaming, or art? In some cases, access adds another layer of worth, as certain NFTs grant holders ongoing benefits such as entry into exclusive communities or access to new content releases.

Social trends can shift NFT prices dramatically. When a collection captures public attention, it can evolve into a status symbol of digital ownership. The Bored Ape Yacht Club, for example, became far more than a set of digital images. Owners connected through private events, online communities, and a shared sense of identity. The excitement attracted celebrities and everyday investors alike. However, not every collection enjoys lasting success, and prices can fall sharply once the spotlight fades.

The ways people use NFTs go well beyond art collecting. Artists have found new ways to monetize digital works. Instead of selling files that can be copied endlessly, they mint NFTs and sell them in limited supply. Buyers enjoy not just bragging rights but also confidence that their purchase is genuine and recorded. Musicians, too, have begun releasing albums or concert tickets in NFT form, creating new income streams and fan engagement models. Platforms like Royal let fans buy a share of music streaming rights as NFTs.

In gaming, NFTs have created fresh economics inside virtual worlds. In Axie Infinity, a game with a booming NFT economy; players buy, sell, and breed digital creatures called "Axies." These creatures are NFTs that players actually own, trade, or use in battles. Sometimes, a rare Axie or in-game tool gains real-world value, with sales crossing tens of thousands of dollars. Players can make money by selling what they earn or find in the game, blurring old lines between entertainment and investing.

NFTs also serve in membership and rewards. Groups like Proof Collective or VeeFriends grant NFT holders access to closed communities, network events, or annual conferences. Instead of a printed card, members show their digital wallet as their ticket. This approach helps clubs prove membership quickly and add features over time, such as special content or meetups for NFT owners only.

Ongoing experiments in utility NFTs are changing ticketing and event access. Some companies now issue event passes as NFTs. The owner can resell a ticket safely, because the blockchain proves authenticity and prevents duplication. The original event organizer can even take a share of any resale, a trick that fights scalping and rewards creators.

These examples show both the creative energy and new risks in NFT markets. Ownership, authenticity, hype, and utility mix together, shaping a fast-moving landscape that attracts attention and speculation. NFT investing offers possibilities but demands careful planning. With this foundation, investors can start to think through how to approach NFTs: whether to flip, hold, or seek long-term value, and how to stay safe as they do.

Investment Strategies and Risk Management in NFTs

A solid foundation in NFT concepts paves the way for safer, more confident investing. Before making any moves, it's smart to recognize the unique risks of the NFT space. NFT markets move quickly and attract opportunists. Some projects may disappear overnight, and not all marketplaces offer equal security. Start by sticking to well-known marketplaces like OpenSea, Rarible, or LooksRare, which have established tools and clear user protections. Double-check that any NFT project's creator profile is verified, and look for links to recognized social accounts. Before purchasing, examine smart contract details; public block explorers let you review contract addresses, verify conditions, and spot irregularities.

Community reputation can signal a project's health. Read feedback in Discords, Telegram groups, and Twitter replies. Watch for accounts with only a few posts or sudden boosts in followers; these are red flags for artificial hype. Search for independent reviews or trackers that assess project milestones or reveal past troubles. Always set spending limits and separate funds used for NFT purchases from the money you need for bills or daily expenses. Even the most promising projects carry risk, so only invest what you can afford to lose.

Emotions play a big role in NFT investing. FOMO spikes during high-profile drops, often leading to hurried buying without proper research. Pause before making decisions; even a short wait can prevent regret. Instances of poorly researched projects abound: in some cases, teams promised unique artwork or rare perks, launched with flashy websites, and then vanished after the initial sale. Compare that to buyers who thoroughly checked team backgrounds, confirmed digital signatures, chatted with other collectors, and saw stable project progress; these investments are more likely to grow in value or at least avoid disaster.

Short-term flipping offers a way to profit by buying and selling NFTs in quick succession. This strategy hinges on timing and finding collections primed for attention. Ideal flipping candidates often have limited supply, strong buzz across social media, or feature highly anticipated timed drops. Flippers typically monitor Discord and Twitter for early signs of community excitement, often using NFT analytics tools like Nansen or Icy Tools to spot trending projects. They track mint dates, whitelist opportunities, and pre-sale leaks.

In a typical flipping scenario, an investor sees a surge of genuine chatter about an upcoming collection. By analyzing recent engagement and activity levels, the investor joins before the general public. If they secure an NFT at mint price, they list it for resale at the first peak of interest, sometimes within hours. Gas fees (transaction costs on the Ethereum network) can eat into profits, so flippers monitor network congestion and set firm price targets to keep trades worthwhile.

Flipping is not without its pitfalls. Prices can plunge just as quickly as they rise, locking up funds in unwanted NFTs. Slow secondary sales may also mean assets cannot be liquidated in time. By setting entry and exit rules, flippers can minimize chasing sudden shifts, and calculating costs in advance helps them avoid unprofitable trades.

Some investors lean toward holding NFTs over longer periods, believing that certain collections or items will increase in value slowly but steadily. Long-term strategies focus on assets with meaningful utility, established creators, and highly engaged communities. NFTs tied to game economies, recurring member perks, or evolving digital art often see gradual and sustained appreciation. Buyers dive into project roadmaps, check the professional credentials of the development team, and watch for regular updates or expanding perks.

The quality of art, development of features, and growth of exclusive benefits contribute strongly to an NFT's future appeal. Holding early in projects like CryptoPunks or Bored Ape Yacht Club allowed collectors to benefit from rising collector interest and added member experiences. These gains were not immediate but built over months, even years, as communities flourished and teams continued to deliver.

Patient analysis is vital before committing to long-term holds. Study how project goals align with delivery, and make sure the creators communicate transparently. Some long-term investors split their portfolio, reserving a portion for blue-chip NFTs and another for newer speculative projects with strong teams.

Comparing flipping and holding, the two approaches serve different types of investors. Flipping demands constant research, a quick reaction to trends, and an appetite for high risk and transaction fees. The rewards can be immediate, but losses come just as fast. Holding needs in-depth vetting, long-term patience, and a willingness to wait for value to emerge. It may carry less day-to-day stress but asks for trust in a project's ongoing life.

Think honestly about your own risk tolerance, time, and financial plans. If rapid trading suits your style and you can accept swift ups and downs, flipping could work for you. If you'd rather bet on the steady rise of carefully chosen projects, long-term holding may fit better. Blending both approaches or starting small with one can allow for learning and growth without overextending, making NFT investing a more controlled and informed process.

Now that you understand the core ideas behind NFTs, their uniqueness, value factors, and range of uses, you are better prepared to decide whether they fit into your investment strategy. NFTs offer exciting opportunities but also carry distinct risks in a market that evolves quickly. Whether you aim for short-term profits or long-term growth, success depends on careful research and a clear plan. By staying objective, verifying projects thoroughly, and aligning your strategy with your goals and risk tolerance, you can navigate the NFT world with confidence and build a crypto portfolio that supports your path to financial freedom.

CHAPTER 17
WALLETS, EXCHANGES, AND TOOLS YOU NEED

Have you ever wondered how to safely buy and store cryptocurrency without falling prey to scams or losing your assets? Are you unsure whether to use a centralized platform that feels more familiar or a decentralized option that offers greater control? Maybe you're curious about which tools can help you track your investments and protect your digital wealth as the market moves rapidly. These are common questions for anyone stepping into the world of crypto, especially when the choices seem overwhelming and the risks real.

This chapter will guide you through the essential decisions and tools needed to build a strong foundation in cryptocurrency investing. You'll learn about different types of exchanges and wallets, how each fits various goals and comfort levels, and practical steps to secure your holdings. We'll also explore helpful apps for tracking your portfolio and staying informed, along with best practices to keep your investments safe from threats. By the end, you'll have a clearer understanding of the must-have resources and security habits that make confident, smart crypto investing possible.

Exchanges and Secure Wallet Choices

Centralized and decentralized exchanges shape how you buy, sell, and hold cryptocurrency. Understanding the difference between these two options is the first step to making informed decisions about your portfolio.

A centralized exchange, or CEX, works a bit like a crypto bank. You sign up for an account, usually with a photo ID and personal information. The platform holds your funds, matches buyers and sellers, and lets you trade digital assets for fiat currency or other cryptocurrencies with the click of a button. Trusted names in the CEX space include Coinbase, Binance, and Kraken. These platforms make it easy to deposit dollars, euros, or other traditional currencies, which can streamline your first steps into crypto.

Centralized exchanges often appeal to new investors because of their user-friendly design, strong customer support, and sense of familiarity. These platforms hold your crypto for you, so you don't have to worry about managing keys or backup phrases right away. High trading volume means you can usually buy or sell quickly, even during busy market hours. CEXs are heavily regulated, so they follow regional laws on consumer protection and anti-money laundering. That comes with the trade-off of personal identity disclosure, account monitoring, and sometimes account freezes.

Decentralized exchanges, or DEXs, trade all that structure for freedom. DEXs are peer-to-peer marketplaces, closer to a neighborhood swap meet than a bank. You trade directly with other users through your own crypto wallet, and there's no central company holding your funds or collecting your identity. Popular DEXs include Uniswap and PancakeSwap. They're accessible through an internet browser or mobile app, connecting directly to blockchain networks like Ethereum or Binance Smart Chain.

DEXs give you more control and privacy. You don't have to register with your name or email, instead, you link your own wallet and start trading. These platforms often carry new or rare coins that never make it to big exchanges. The flip side is that you're responsible for securing your own funds and navigating sometimes complicated user interfaces. Transaction fees can spike during busy periods, and support typically comes from the community rather than a help desk.

Choosing between a CEX and a DEX depends on your comfort with technology, privacy priorities, and tolerance for risk:

When to consider a CEX:

- You want an easy start with fiat money
- You value customer support and strong account security features
- You trade large amounts or need high liquidity

When a DEX might fit you better:

- You want privacy and personal control
- You're interested in hard-to-find coins
- You're willing to manage your own wallet security and accept responsibility for mistakes

Wallets are the next foundation. In crypto, a wallet is where you store your digital keys, which are required to access your assets. Every wallet type has trade-offs, and picking the right one depends on what you value most: convenience, security, or long-term safety.

Hot wallets connect to the internet. They come as browser extensions, mobile apps, or desktop programs. Examples include MetaMask, Trust Wallet, and Coinbase Wallet. Hot wallets are convenient for daily trading, especially for people who frequently buy and sell coins and want to react quickly to market changes. They make moving funds simple but also expose users to hacks, scams, and device theft. Keeping large sums in a hot wallet increases risk. There are many stories of investors who lost all their crypto through phishing attacks or malware because their wallets remained connected online.

Cold wallets store your crypto keys offline. The simplest version is a paper wallet, which is just a printed document with your key codes. More common are hardware wallets, small USB-like devices such as Ledger and Trezor. They remain offline except when plugged in to sign a transaction, eliminating most online threats. Hardware wallets offer the best balance between accessibility and security for serious investors. Some people have lost access to exchanges but recovered their funds using a hardware backup, while others lost everything because they kept their crypto online.

Before choosing a wallet, consider three things: control of your private keys (are you the only one who has them?), backup options (can you recover your wallet if your computer fails?), and security features such as two-factor authentication or passphrase protection.

A strong foundation built on reliable exchanges and wallets forms the base for everything you do in crypto. Once you have these in place, adding tools like tracking apps, tax software, or portfolio analytics becomes easier and safer. Each layer adds both strength and flexibility, beginning with how and where you store and trade your assets.

Essential Crypto Tools and Security Practices

Everyday crypto investors depend on a range of tools to keep track of markets, manage assets, spot fraud, and maintain control. One of the first essentials in any toolkit is a trusted market data aggregator. For this purpose, sites like CoinMarketCap and CoinGecko exist. With these resources, you can look up any coin, check real-time prices, and compare trading volumes and liquidity across exchanges. Each site lets you dig deeper by showing market cap rankings, historical charts, project summaries, and links to official websites or contract addresses. This makes it simple to avoid lookalike coins or scam tokens with similar names.

Setting price alerts on these sites is a practical step. Imagine seeing a sudden price pump on social media; a quick check on CoinGecko helps you see actual changes, price history, volume patterns, and whether the move is happening across major exchanges or just one illiquid spot. If you're waiting to buy or sell, these tools' alert systems let you set target prices. You'll get a push notification or email the moment your conditions are met, rather than reacting impulsively to headlines or FOMO (fear of missing out).

Portfolio tracker apps are another must-have. With dozens of coins and wallets, you need a clear snapshot of everything you own. Apps like Blockfolio or Delta connect directly to your wallets and exchanges. Instead of logging in to five separate accounts, you see all your balances, total net worth, and performance charts in one place. This ease is useful during wild market swings. For example, when Bitcoin declines by 15% overnight and you want to see your overall exposure or how your altcoins are holding up, a tracker app answers instantly.

Many portfolio trackers offer more than just basic summaries. Look for features like automatic price updating, built-in tax reports, and detailed charts showing unrealized gains and losses. When tax season arrives, a tracker with an integrated reporting tool can save days of frustration. All transfers, swaps, and trades are logged automatically if you connect your wallets using public 'read-only' keys or APIs. No need to share private keys or give up security.

Setting Up Tracking and Research Tools

Here's a short step-by-step guide to integrating trackers and data sources:

1. Download a portfolio app from the official website or app store.
2. Choose the 'add wallet' or 'add exchange' option.
3. If the app supports wallet syncing, paste in your public (not private) wallet address.
4. For exchange syncing, log in using a secure 'read-only' API key, never a withdrawal-enabled one.

5. Assign a name to the app, and observe as it automatically imports balances and trades.
6. Set price alerts for coins you follow.
7. Activate two-factor authentication on the app.

For market research, aggregators like Messari or CryptoPanic combine news headlines, project updates, and even developer activity. You see the source and timestamp for every alert. When rumors break, these platforms let you verify news with a single glance. On-chain analytics sites like Glassnode reveal investor behavior, large wallet movements, and unusual activity, signaling possible pump-and-dump schemes.

Social media monitoring also matters. Crypto markets move on tweets and Reddit threads. Aggregators filter the noise by pulling key updates or sometimes warning of coordinated 'shilling' campaigns. By collecting news from official Twitter or Medium feeds, these tools help you distinguish between real project announcements and viral rumors.

Security Best Practices

Security is the foundation for protecting your investments. Start with strong, unique passwords for each exchange, wallet, and app. Use a password manager like Bitwarden or 1Password, which generates and remembers complex passwords so you don't reuse the same one.

Always enable two-factor authentication (2FA). Google Authenticator or Authy is the gold standard here. Authentication by SMS is vulnerable to SIM swapping, so stick with app-based codes. Every login and transfer should prompt for this second code, making it almost impossible for a hacker to access your account with only your password.

Only download wallet software, portfolio apps, and extensions from official download links or recognized app stores. Fake apps or malicious browser add-ons are a common trick; a single download can steal your coins.

Phishing attacks are common, so check every website address before entering passwords. Bookmark important sites, and ignore suspicious emails or direct messages offering unexpected giveaways or claiming wallet issues. Never share backup phrases or private keys, not even with customer support.

Backup Strategies

Losing access to a wallet can mean losing everything. Keep written backup phrases in a safe offline location (never digital notes or cloud storage). Use password managers to store exchange logins, but store wallet seed phrases on paper or a hardware device, separate from your computer.

If you use multi-signature wallets or hardware wallets, keep backup devices or written instructions in different safe locations. Let a trusted family member know where the backup is, just in case.

In volatile or uncertain times, these practices help remove stress from investing. A security mistake or app failure feels far less frightening when you have reliable backups and trusted tools in place. Tools work best when combined with disciplined habits, helping you avoid panic, scams, and unnecessary losses while giving you the confidence to grow and protect your crypto wealth.

Now that you understand the key choices between exchanges and wallets, along with the essential tools and security habits needed to manage your crypto safely, you're ready to take confident steps into this dynamic market. Building a strong foundation means you can focus on growing your portfolio without fear of common pitfalls like scams or lost assets. With these basics in place, you can explore advanced strategies to diversify your holdings, track your progress effectively, and protect your investments with smart backups and alerts. This chapter sets the stage for you to move forward thoughtfully and securely, turning curiosity into real financial opportunity in the world of cryptocurrency.

CHAPTER 18
BUILDING A PROFITABLE CRYPTO PORTFOLIO

Many people jump into cryptocurrency expecting quick wins, only to find themselves caught in a rollercoaster of unpredictable prices and risky bets. The truth is, building real wealth with crypto isn't about chasing the latest hype or betting everything on one coin. It requires a thoughtful strategy that balances growth potential with risk management, especially in a market known for wild swings.

This chapter will guide you through creating a crypto portfolio designed for steady, methodical wealth growth. You'll learn how to combine reliable core assets with carefully chosen satellites to match your comfort level with risk. We'll explore practical ways to diversify across coins and sectors, use different investment methods, and manage your holdings over time. By the end, you'll have a clear plan tailored to your financial goals—whether you want conservative stability or are ready to take bigger chances while protecting your capital.

Understanding Portfolio Foundations: Core and Satellite Assets with Sample Strategies

A strong crypto portfolio does not rely on a single asset or short-term hunches. Investors use a smart approach called core-satellite investing to structure their holdings for both growth and stability.

This strategy divides your assets into two types. The core forms the backbone, made up of the largest and most established cryptocurrencies such as Bitcoin and Ethereum. Satellite assets surround the core and include altcoins, DeFi tokens, NFTs, and newer projects that carry higher risk. Grouping your investments in this way allows you to pursue growth while protecting your capital from the sharp fluctuations of the crypto market.

Core assets hold a key place in this structure because of their history and broad acceptance. Bitcoin is recognized as the first and most widely adopted cryptocurrency, known for its limited supply and strong network effects. Ethereum serves as the main platform for smart contracts and decentralized applications, forming the base for much of the innovation in the crypto space today. Both have survived multiple market cycles, proving their durability and importance within the broader digital economy. Holding a healthy share of your portfolio in such coins means you are anchored to assets with solid liquidity, brand recognition, and ongoing developer support.

Satellite assets, on the other hand, introduce excitement and potential for quick gains, but with them comes more risk. These assets include well-known altcoins beyond Bitcoin and Ethereum, smaller network coins, tokens powering specific dApps, and even collectibles like NFTs. Sometimes, satellites can multiply in value in a short period; think of tokens that surge after a new protocol or game draws market attention. Still, most satellites are more experimental or tied to a single trend, which makes them unpredictable. If things go wrong, you protect most of your capital by only investing a small part of your portfolio.

This division is not just for safety. It actively supports your long-term returns. Core assets can help smooth out ups and downs in the crypto market, giving you time to wait for the right moments with your satellites. If some speculative bets pay off, you have room to lock in profits and cycle gains back into your core, strengthening your base over time. If satellites dip or fail, your core can prevent the entire portfolio from collapsing. Altogether, you follow a plan, not a gambling streak.

Example Portfolios for Different Risk Levels

Some investors want maximum stability and steady growth. For a conservative profile, a portfolio might look like this:

Core (80%)

- 50% Bitcoin (BTC)
- 30% Ethereum (ETH)

Satellite (20%)

- 10% Binance Coin (BNB)
- 5% Polygon (MATIC)
- 5% Chainlink (LINK)

This combination allows the core to maintain its value during challenging times, while satellites provide additional growth opportunities without jeopardizing your base wealth.

For those comfortable with more risk, preference shifts a bit:

Core (60%)

- 35% Bitcoin (BTC)
- 25% Ethereum (ETH)

Satellite (40%)

- 10% Solana (SOL)
- 10% Avalanche (AVAX)
- 10% Uniswap (UNI)
- 10% in new DeFi or metaverse projects

This kind of balance meets the needs of someone who believes in crypto's future but wants to avoid betting it all on one horse. You can tap into fresh trends and sectors while still holding fast to the strongest coins.

For those who enjoy taking bigger swings on rapid gains and are ready to handle losses, an aggressive approach might resemble the following:

Core (40%)

- 20% Bitcoin (BTC)
- 20% Ethereum (ETH)

Satellite (60%)

- 15% in trending metaverse tokens
- 15% in small-cap altcoins with growth buzz
- 10% in early-stage DeFi protocols
- 10% in select NFTs
- 10% in ecosystem tokens, like Fantom (FTM) or Cosmos (ATOM)

This portfolio backs up its moonshot chasing with enough core to soften a hard market crash, making it more disciplined than going "all in" on unproven coins. It draws boundaries, so even when chasing high rewards, the risk of ruin is limited.

How Core-Satellite Investing Works During Market Shocks

Imagine an investor who held only hyped altcoins during a sharp correction, say, a 60% drop in new project prices over weeks. They could lose much of their principal and then hesitate or sell off in panic, missing the recovery. Someone using a core-satellite structure, on the other hand, might find their Bitcoin and Ethereum holdings drop too, but with much smaller drawdowns. The core assets are more likely to recover, providing a cushion, while at least some satellites might bounce strongly later, letting the investor rebalance when the storm has passed.

The concept of core and satellite provides structure and stability in a market characterized by swift fluctuations. Once this basic balance is set, another question grows: how do you pick the best satellites, and how can you make your portfolio even more resilient and full of opportunity by diversifying within those satellites? Sectors, strategies, and asset types offer many new ways forward.

Implementing Diversification and Ongoing Management Techniques

Step-by-step portfolio construction is just the start. Maximizing returns and limiting risk come from weaving together several types of diversification and sticking with steady management methods.

Spreading risk by coin type matters for crypto more than in most markets. Lean too heavily on large coins like Bitcoin or Ethereum, and performance may mirror only market trends. If you invest all your money in small-cap coins in the hopes of achieving a significant return, the unpredictable fluctuations could potentially disrupt your goals or even completely erase your progress. The sweet spot often lies in blending these: large-cap coins for their staying power with doses of mid-cap and small-cap coins for upside potential.

A sample allocation could look like this:

- 60% in large-cap coins: Bitcoin, Ethereum
- 25% in mid-cap coins: Solana, Polygon, Avalanche
- 15% in small-cap coins: new DeFi or gaming tokens

Here, the majority sits in assets with long histories and active communities. This anchors the portfolio against sharp downturns. The mid- and small-cap slices let you tap projects at earlier stages, which are risky but offer higher growth. If something goes wrong with a small-cap, losses won't sink the whole portfolio.

Coins are only one way to diversify. Crypto spreads across sectors that behave differently as the market changes. Relying on only one segment, maybe all "layer 1" blockchains like Ethereum and its peers could leave you exposed if that sector faces trouble, such as network congestion, major hacks, or regulation. Layer 2 solutions, made to improve speed and reduce fees, do not always move in step with layer 1s. Decentralized finance (DeFi) protocols might stumble during market fear but bounce back on innovation or adoption. NFT and gaming tokens show unique cycles, often growing during wider market slumps, which provides a degree of balance.

A robust spread could cover:

- Layer 1 blockchains: Ethereum, Cardano
- Layer 2 solutions: Polygon, Optimism
- DeFi: Aave, Uniswap, Curve
- NFTs/gaming: Axie Infinity, Decentraland
- Infrastructure: Chainlink, Filecoin

When the government cracks down on DeFi lending, DeFi coins may tumble while layer 1 blockchains or NFT platforms show resilience. The opposite might happen if NFTs lose hype but financial activity on blockchains remains strong. Spreading bets means losses in one area won't always translate to losses everywhere.

Another dimension is investment methods. It's one thing to buy and hold coins. Doing only that can miss opportunities when trends shift. Adding short- or medium-term trading lets you react to market excitement or price dips. Some coins, like Ethereum or Solana, offer "staking," locking coins up to help network security and earn a yield. Others supply income through DeFi lending or yield farming. Each method has its rewards and tradeoffs.

Suppose you allocate:

- 70% to long-term holds like Bitcoin and Ethereum
- 20% to trading positions—buying mid-cap coins on price dips, selling after gains
- 10% to income: staking Cardano, lending USDC for interest

In this mix, core assets ride long-term growth, trades aim for quicker profit, and staking or lending produces extra yield regardless of price moves. If trading hits a losing streak, steady income from staking helps smooth results.

Ongoing management gives shape to these diligent choices. Portfolios drift as prices surge or dive. Left unchecked, allocations meant for balance soon become lopsided. Say Ethereum doubles and now makes up 40% instead of the planned 25%. This exposes a portfolio to higher single-asset risk. Good investors bring it back in line with "rebalancing," selling some winners and topping up laggards.

Two common, practical ways to rebalance:

- **Time-based approach**: Once every month or quarter, review allocations and adjust as needed.
- **Threshold-based approach**: Whenever an asset shifts more than, say, 5% from its target allocation, rebalance only those parts.

For example, if DeFi coins surge to 30% of your holdings (from a 20% target), sell part for stablecoins or other assets. This keeps each category in check, protects against shock losses, and lets profits from one lucky run fuel new bets elsewhere.

Managing a portfolio is not just about adding or removing coins but judging what works. Several crypto portfolio trackers allow connections to exchanges and wallets, making it much simpler to check your exposure, track gains, and log losses. Even a manual spreadsheet with columns for entry price, amount, and sector can help.

A quick review each month, checking which sectors win, which lag, and where allocations drifted, unlocks insights. Spot a coin that always drags your totals down, and you can cut it. Notice that gaming tokens rose while everything else slid? You'll see trends to catch next time, keeping you close to your goals and steering with confidence.

Now that you understand how to build a well-structured crypto portfolio using the core-satellite approach, tailored to your risk comfort and goals, you're ready to put this knowledge into practice. By balancing stable, established coins with carefully chosen growth opportunities and maintaining ongoing management like diversification and rebalancing, you can navigate the highs and lows of the crypto market with confidence and discipline. This methodical strategy protects your investment while providing opportunities for significant gains. As you move forward, remember that success in crypto investing comes from staying informed, adapting thoughtfully, and sticking to a plan, not chasing every trend. With these tools at your disposal, you can increase your wealth over time in a steady and intelligent manner.

CHAPTER 19
PROFIT STRATEGIES – FROM HODLING TO DAY TRADING

Profit in the world of cryptocurrency isn't about luck or timing the market perfectly, it's about understanding different approaches and aligning them with your own goals, temperament, and daily life. Many people think there's a single right way to invest: buy and hold forever or trade rapidly to chase every price move. In reality, the best strategy depends on who you are, how much time you have, and how you handle risk and stress.

This chapter explores the range of methods available, from holding assets patiently over years to actively trading based on short-term momentum, helping you find the approach that fits you best. It also offers practical guidance on managing risks, setting rules for your trades, and developing habits that protect your investments and your peace of mind. Whether you're new to crypto or ready to take your investing to the next level, these insights will help you build a plan designed for steady, sustainable profits.

Investment Styles: HODLing vs. Active Trading Methods

Imagine a spectrum of crypto investing styles, on one end sits the quiet patience of the HODLer, and on the other, the constant motion of the momentum trader. Each path reflects a different way to interact with the chaos and opportunity of crypto markets, each with strengths and pitfalls. Choosing a method asks you to consider what matches your mindset, your life, and your goals, much more than chasing whatever strategy is trending on social media.

HODLing, a playful twist on "hold," stands for "Hold On for Dear Life." The idea is simple; buy a crypto asset you believe in and keep it for years, resisting the urge to sell during wild price swings. Like a seedling, you nurture it, knowing it may seem weak but could grow strong and useful. This approach appeals to those with demanding jobs or tight schedules, people who prefer to set things up once, then step away. The main attraction is the simplicity. There's less pressure to time the market or constantly follow price charts. It can be tax-friendly since long-term holdings usually get better treatment in many countries. On the downside, the ride can be rough. Your investment may shrink by half during market corrections, testing your patience and nerves. Opportunity cost becomes real if crypto stagnates while other markets or investments grow. The risk here isn't just market drops but the psychological toll of seeing your portfolio down double digits for months.

Swing trading sits in the middle. Think of it as catching a train partway through its journey. Instead of riding out every bump, you aim to get on and off near the peaks and valleys of shorter trends. Swing traders look for patterns such as prices bouncing between two levels or a big move beginning to slow, then open trades that last for a few days or weeks. Unlike HODLing, swing trading requires more involvement, including frequent market checks and learning to use tools like moving averages, support and resistance zones, and candlestick patterns.

The reward is the chance to profit from the smaller ups and downs without facing the full weight of major market crashes. However, this method comes with more emotional swings, since quick reversals can erase gains. It suits people who enjoy analysis, have time to review charts after work, and feel comfortable making moderately paced decisions. Imagine a lawyer who checks the market in the evening, studies a few key indicators, and makes one or two trades each month while keeping both stress and risk under control.

Trend trading stretches the timeframe further. The goal is to recognize when an asset begins moving steadily in one direction and stay with that trend until signs of change appear. It's like following a river's current, letting the flow carry you instead of fighting every turn. Trend traders create clear rules, such as buying only when the price stays above a certain moving average or selling when specific indicators turn negative. This approach reduces the noise and stress of short-term movements. It requires patience but also alertness, since the market can sometimes trick traders with false reversals. People with steady routines, such as teachers, often prefer this style because it allows them to check the market once a day, hold positions for weeks or months, and avoid the fast pace of daily trading.

Momentum trading sits at the other end of the spectrum. Momentum traders look for coins that are already moving quickly and jump in to ride the surge, aiming to sell before the momentum fades. Imagine surfing; you have to paddle hard, catch the wave at the right moment, and exit as soon as it loses strength. This strategy demands constant attention to price charts, quick decision-making, and strict loss-control rules. The potential rewards are rapid profits, but the risks are equally fast. It appeals to people who enjoy excitement, react well under pressure, and can handle volatility. Picture a freelance marketer with flexible hours, scanning the markets for sudden opportunities and thriving on the high energy of fast trades.

To narrow in on your fit, weigh your schedule, comfort with risk, stress resilience, and desire for involvement. Ask yourself:

- Do you want to check prices once a week, or does the idea of daily action attract you?
- Are you patient when money is tied up for months, or do short-term results keep you motivated?

- How well do you cope with swings in value, or the sting of selling too soon or too late?
- Do technical charts sound interesting, or do you zone out at the mention of "support levels"?

Once you've spotted your place on this spectrum, building discipline and using practical trading tools will help you lock in profits and protect yourself from big mistakes. The coming pages break down these essential strategies—stop-loss orders, risk controls, and mindset habits—to reinforce success, no matter which style you've chosen.

Practical Steps for Safe and Sustainable Profits

Buying and selling cryptocurrency comes with risks that skilled investors recognize and control. Setting up a stop-loss is one of the most practical ways to protect yourself from sudden downturns. A stop-loss is a preset order that tells your exchange to sell an asset if its price drops below a certain level. This tool functions similarly to insurance; if the value falls below your set limit, it automatically triggers a sale, allowing you to minimize your losses without any hesitation or panic. To set a stop-loss on most crypto exchanges, first decide your threshold. For example, if you buy Bitcoin at $30,000, you might want to risk no more than 10%. You would set your stop-loss at $27,000. On many exchanges, you click 'Stop-Limit' or 'Stop Order,' input your trigger price ($27,000), and specify the quantity to sell. You can also base your stop-loss on support levels by identifying price points where an asset has "bounced back" before and placing your order just below this zone. Percentage limits protect you from emotional overreactions, while support-based stops account for market behavior. No stop-loss is perfect, but skipping this step is the surest path to letting one disastrous trade wreck your portfolio.

Emotional highs and lows often lead to poor trading decisions. Crypto markets move quickly, inviting both fear and greed. When prices drop sharply, many traders panic and sell everything. When coins surge, fear of missing out causes others to buy too late or at inflated prices. Recognizing these emotional triggers is your first line of defense. Maybe your pulse races as prices fall, or you find yourself checking charts every few minutes after a big rally. These are signs that emotion, not logic, is guiding your actions. Planning your trades in advance helps reduce this influence. Write down your entry and exit points, and keep a trading journal to record what you intended to do versus what actually happened, along with how you felt during each step. For example, if your plan is to buy Ethereum at $2,000 and sell at $2,300 but the price hits $2,400, stick to your strategy, or at least review your plan before reacting. Building this habit prevents impulsive moves that lead to regret.

Trading around the clock or monitoring assets constantly will drain your focus. Many new traders burn out quickly by spending late nights glued to screens, trapped in a cycle of stress and rushed decisions. Fatigue leads to mistakes and risky choices. Setting boundaries is essential. Limit trading to specific hours and then walk away. Schedule short breaks to reset your mind. After a tough loss or a major win, take time off to cool down. This pause helps prevent emotional reactions such as "revenge trading," when traders try to recover losses immediately. If you notice anxiety at certain times, like when the market opens, turn off notifications and check prices only at set moments, such as lunchtime or after work. Over time, these habits protect your focus, decision-making, and peace of mind.

Tax season can also catch unprepared investors off guard. Every time you sell crypto, even when exchanging one coin for another, you may trigger a taxable event. This means each transaction must be reported on your tax return. Gains fall into two categories: short term, for assets held one year or less, and long term, for those held longer than a year. Short term gains are usually taxed at your regular income rate, while long term gains often qualify for a lower rate. For example, if you buy Litecoin for $5,000 and sell it after eleven months for $6,000, you owe short term capital gains tax on the $1,000 profit. Holding for thirteen months could qualify for a lower rate. Frequent trading increases the number of transactions and receipts to track, so using crypto tax software or hiring a professional can help prevent costly errors and audits. Staying organized from the beginning makes tax time far less stressful.

Building wealth through crypto should not look or feel like a casino trip. Gambling means chasing quick wins, ignoring losses, and making impulsive "all-in" bets. Successful investors do the opposite. They pick a small set of coins, research carefully, and set clear entry and exit rules for every trade. They use stop-losses as guardrails. Realistic expectations matter, aiming for steady, small gains and seeing losses as learning tools. Start by selecting one or two coins, not ten. Decide when you're willing to enter a trade, where your exit and stop-loss should be, and how much risk is comfortable for your finances. Track every trade in a notebook or app. Over time, review your patterns and adjust. Small, consistent efforts build into solid results, protecting you from both wild swings and burnout. The goal is control, not chance. By committing to these steps, you set yourself up for progress that lasts.

Now that you understand the spectrum of crypto investing from steady HODLing to active momentum trading and the tools to manage risk and emotions, you're equipped to choose a strategy that fits your lifestyle and goals. Remember, success comes from discipline, clear planning, and learning from each trade, not from chasing quick wins or following hype. As you move forward, keep refining your approach with practical habits like setting stop-losses, limiting stress, and staying organized for taxes. With this foundation, you can confidently build a balanced crypto portfolio designed for sustainable growth and long-term wealth.

CHAPTER 20

PASSIVE INCOME IN CRYPTO – STAKING, YIELD FARMING & MORE

Have you ever wondered how people turn their cryptocurrency holdings into steady streams of income without constantly buying and selling? What if your digital coins could work quietly in the background, earning rewards while you focus on other things? If the idea of making money from crypto sounds exciting but confusing, you're not alone. Many investors are curious about ways to generate passive income through blockchain technology but hesitate because the landscape feels complicated and risky. Knowing where to start, which strategies are effective, and how to avoid common pitfalls can significantly impact the difference between missed opportunities and intelligent growth. This chapter will help you see how practical crypto income methods fit together, revealing paths that suit your goals and comfort level so you can build a more confident approach to earning with digital assets.

Getting Started with Staking, Yield Farming, Lending Platforms, and Liquidity Pools

Staking opens a door for crypto holders to make their coins work for them. By locking up, or "staking," coins on certain blockchains, users help secure the network and earn regular rewards in return. Imagine someone with 10 Solana tokens. Instead of keeping them idle, they deposit these Solana into a platform like Kraken or Coinbase. After a simple setup, rewards begin to appear in the account. Staking is accessible because many exchanges make it a one-click action for popular coins such as Ethereum, Cardano, or Solana.

How to Start Staking

1. Pick a coin supported by staking (such as Ethereum, Cardano, Solana).
2. Set up an account on a trusted exchange (Coinbase and Kraken are good options).
3. Secure your account with strong passwords and two-factor authentication.
4. Buy or deposit your chosen coin.
5. Find the staking section and follow the steps to stake your coins.
6. Review any lockup terms—some coins allow instant withdrawal, others may have a time delay.

Staking on centralized exchanges is usually more user-friendly than using third-party wallets or validators, but the tradeoff can be higher fees or less control over advanced settings. When comparing platforms, Coinbase is known for simple interfaces and low entry requirements, while Kraken offers a wider variety of coins and detailed performance stats. Watch out for unknown platforms with limited reviews or no proof of regular audits.

Staking Best Practices

- Always stake using a reputable, regulated exchange or a well-known decentralized wallet.
- Do not stake everything at once; start with a small amount to understand how the process works.
- Read the coin's staking lockup rules to avoid being surprised by withdrawal delays.

Now, let's look at yield farming. This strategy uses decentralized finance (DeFi) protocols to generate income by lending tokens or offering liquidity to pools. When you farm yield, you earn extra tokens or fees in exchange for making your own coins available. For example, suppose you have some USD Coin (USDC) and Ethereum (ETH). You head to a platform like Yearn Finance or PancakeSwap, connect a wallet such as MetaMask, and then deposit equal values of both coins into a liquidity pool. This pool lets others swap one token for another, and you earn a slice of the transaction fees.

How to Yield Farm

1. Set up a wallet like MetaMask or Trust Wallet.
2. Transfer coins that you want to farm (for example, USDC and ETH).
3. Research pools on platforms like Yearn Finance, Uniswap, or PancakeSwap.
4. Connect your wallet to the platform.
5. Supply your tokens as instructed.
6. Monitor your earnings and learn about risks like impermanent loss.

Uniswap works well for Ethereum-based tokens with a busy trading environment. PancakeSwap focuses on the Binance Smart Chain, which may offer lower fees. Beginners should avoid platforms with high annual percentage rates but vague reputations or confusing interfaces.

Yield Farming Best Practices

- Check if the protocol has passed third-party audits.
- Never deposit funds into contracts without clear history or transparent team backgrounds.
- Beware of coins with massive rewards that seem unsustainable over time.

The next approach is crypto lending. Here, you lend your coins through special platforms and earn interest as others borrow them. Well-known projects like Aave and Compound act as intermediaries between lenders and borrowers. If you own DAI or USDC, you deposit these stablecoins into the platform and receive regular interest payments. Getting started on Aave or Compound only takes a wallet with compatible tokens, no long applications or credit checks.

Steps to Start Lending

1. Set up a wallet (MetaMask or Ledger).
2. Acquire tokens like DAI, USDC, or ETH.
3. Visit a lending platform such as Aave or Compound.
4. Connect your wallet, select "Deposit," and follow steps to lend your tokens.
5. Monitor your rate of return in real-time through the platform's dashboard.

Aave and Compound offer slightly different borrower profiles and interest calculations, but both are easy to use for new users. Watch for hidden fees, platform hacks, and any unproven new lending protocols.

Lending Best Practices

- Stick with projects with a long track record and regular security audits.
- Keep an eye on platform health metrics to spot trouble early.
- Do not lend out coins that you cannot afford to lock up for months.

Finally, liquidity pools attract users looking to share in trading fees. When you act as a liquidity provider, you combine two kinds of tokens in a pool such as ETH and USDC on Uniswap. Each time someone swaps, you earn part of the fees generated. Alice, who has 1 ETH and 1,800 USDC, provides both to the ETH-USDC pool. After a month, she checks the pool and sees she has earned about $20 in fees, minus a slight change in her balances due to trading activity.

When choosing a pool, consider token popularity, fees, and the risk of "impermanent loss," where token values shift. Platforms like Uniswap and PancakeSwap are ideal for first-timers, with simple instructions and helpful stats.

Liquidity Pool Best Practices

- Always research the pool's trade volume and previous returns.
- Provide liquidity with stablecoins first to minimize extreme price swings.
- Withdraw tokens promptly if the pool experiences sudden spikes or hacks.

While earning passive income in cryptocurrency opens up new possibilities, the risks and returns are always changing. To succeed, prioritize safety and risk awareness as much as potential rewards.

Evaluating DeFi Returns, Risks, and Real Examples of Passive Earnings

Diving into DeFi income streams goes beyond just pressing a few buttons to start earning. Unlike staking a single token for a fixed reward or earning interest from a traditional savings account, returns in DeFi shift constantly. When you open a DeFi protocol and see an annual percentage yield, or APY, of 20%, that number isn't fixed in place. It can swing higher or lower by the week, day, and sometimes the hour. For someone used to a 2% fixed-interest rate from a bank or an advertised 5% staking return from a blue-chip crypto, this kind of movement might feel wild and unpredictable.

The reasons for this variability run deeper than simple market ups and downs. Every DeFi platform draws from pools of tokens provided by real users. If more liquidity floods in, yields might drop as rewards are split among extra participants. When incentives spike to attract fresh capital, maybe in the form of bonus tokens or special events, APYs can shoot up, only to drop once those events end. Protocol fees, trading activity, and even outside hype make short-term yields bounce around. This means planning for consistent passive income takes more than just picking whatever offer seems highest in the moment.

Take the example of providing liquidity in a decentralized exchange. Let's say you supply equal amounts of ETH and a stablecoin to a pool. Initially, the APY looks attractive, boosted by trading fees and token incentives. Now, picture a sudden price swing in ETH, up or down. If traders act quickly, you may end up with more of one asset and less of the other, changing the value of your holdings. This "impermanent loss" eats into the returns you were expecting, sometimes wiping out the gains from attractive APYs.

Beyond shifting yields, there's the risk tied to the code itself. A traditional bank has audited systems and government protections. In DeFi, everything runs on smart contracts, automated logic written on a blockchain. If there's a flaw, whether from sloppy programming or a clever attack, funds can disappear in minutes. Stories circulate of protocols losing millions, or all, when attackers spot a loophole. One example is a major decentralized lending platform hit by a flash loan exploit: users saw high APYs, but a bug allowed a hacker to drain the pool before anyone could react. No insurance, no reversal. Funds just gone.

Market risk also carries its own lessons. Imagine earning 50% APY from a new protocol offering shiny new tokens as rewards. If the underlying token doubles in value, your rewards grow even faster. However, the token's price crash could cancel out even high-percentage APYs if it drops by half as the hype fades. Some protocols vanish altogether in a scam, often called a "rug pull," where creators yank all the liquidity, leaving the remaining tokens worthless.

Yet for every story of sudden loss, there are practical ways investors protect their capital and sleep easier. The most reliable start with research. Check whether a platform's smart contracts have been independently audited; a public "seal of approval" means the code got at least a basic safety check. Instead of dumping every dollar into one pool, cautious users spread their holdings across several trusted protocols or asset types. This way, a single bug or market dive won't wipe out everything. Some limit their exposure to any single project, using several wallets or accounts, making tracking easier and risk lower.

Setting a rule to withdraw profits regularly locks in gains. Maybe you decide to withdraw once a week or after hitting a certain target. This buffer helps cushion against sudden dips or panic-inducing hacks. Many investors watch project news, social media, and official updates closely. If a protocol hints at changes, pauses withdrawals, or there's sudden outrage in the community, it could be a red flag to pull funds or pause adding more.

Risk-adjusted returns stay central to smart DeFi moves. Instead of getting tempted by double- or triple-digit APYs, think through what risks you're being paid to take. Higher returns usually mean absorbing bigger swings. For some, stability from large, well-known protocols trumps the dream of sky-high yields, while others experiment on a small scale with riskier projects.

Stories paint the lessons in bold. Take Lisa, who put small sums into a new DeFi farm during a market rally. She tracked APYs daily, doubled her holdings as the coins gained popularity, and harvested profits each week, building up her investment. When the bull run faded, she'd already secured a solid gain, not chasing hype but riding momentum wisely. On the other hand, Chris made a significant investment in a visually appealing new protocol. When the token crashed following a rumored hack, his significant investment disappeared almost overnight. He regrouped, read up on audits, and the next time, split his funds and stayed nimble, losing less when a project hiccuped again.

This world of DeFi passive income rewards those who stay curious, check their assumptions, and treat every protocol as a living experiment. The best results come from small, steady steps, learning as you go, always ready to adjust for what's next on the horizon.

Now that you understand the practical steps and risks involved in staking, yield farming, lending, and providing liquidity, you're better equipped to start generating passive income with cryptocurrency. Building a profitable crypto portfolio requires careful research, patience, and a willingness to learn from real-world experiences. By spreading your investments across trusted platforms and staying alert to market changes and protocol updates, you can balance potential rewards with safety. As you take these first steps, remember that steady progress and risk management will help you turn crypto opportunities into lasting wealth, setting a strong foundation for your financial future.

CHAPTER 21

RISK MANAGEMENT – PROTECTING YOURSELF IN A VOLATILE MARKET

More than half of all cryptocurrency investors lose money within their first year. The volatile nature of crypto markets means prices can soar one day and plummet the next, erasing months of gains in just a few hours. Many newcomers jump in, driven by excitement or fear, only to find themselves caught off guard by sudden drops, scams, or costly mistakes that drain their investments faster than they imagined. Understanding risk is not only about numbers but about knowing how to protect your assets and stay calm when markets become unpredictable. This chapter explores the importance of managing uncertainty wisely and adopting strategies that help you safeguard your investments through the constant ups and downs of crypto.

Managing Volatility and Avoiding Common Mistakes

The world of cryptocurrency never stands still. Prices can jump or fall by 20% or more in a single day. Volatility in crypto means that values can swing wildly in ways that catch investors off guard. Just when things seem to be moving up with confidence, a sudden reversal can erase months of gains overnight. One day, Bitcoin is climbing at record speed; the next, one tweet or government regulation sends it crashing down. Ethereum has seen similar sharp drops after surges that lure newcomers in by the thousands. These gut-wrenching changes are not rare, they're expected.

A black swan event makes chaos even more unpredictable. This is the kind of sudden, rare crisis that no one sees coming, but when it strikes, it changes everything. In May 2021, a wave of negative headlines and announcements from China and Elon Musk caused a one trillion dollar wipeout across the entire crypto market within just a few days. Investors watched helplessly as coins tumbled one after another. In 2014, Mt. Gox, one of the largest Bitcoin exchanges at the time, collapsed after hackers stole hundreds of millions, leaving users with nothing. Events like these often lead to panic, confusion, and rapid losses. Managing risk begins with accepting that large, unexpected swings are part of crypto's nature. The sooner you recognize this reality, the safer your investing journey will be.

Buying crypto isn't just numbers on a screen; it brings strong feelings to the surface. Fear grabs hold after a sudden dip and pushes people to sell, locking in their losses out of panic. Greed comes out when a coin rallies, driving investors to buy more than they should as they dream of untold riches. Euphoria makes one feel invincible after a big win, tempting riskier bets that rarely end well. Panic-selling can turn a simple temporary drop into a permanent wound. Picture an investor who bought a coin at $1, watched it climb to $3, and then fall to $0.90. Driven by fear, they sell near the bottom, missing the rebound a week later, when the price returns to $2.50. Chasing pumps feels exciting until the coin dumps just as fast, leading to regret and doubt. Holding through wild swings without a plan causes stress, exhaustion, and often poor decisions. These emotional swings are natural, but unchecked, they can destroy a beginner's capital.

10 Most Common Mistakes Beginners Make

1. **Investing too much in one coin**

Putting most of your money in a single cryptocurrency can lead to big losses if that coin tanks. For example, many put everything in Luna or other hot tokens, only to see them collapse in price far quicker than expected.

2. **Following hype instead of research**

Social media is full of "can't-lose" recommendations and viral tips. An investor might buy based on a trending hashtag, only to see the price fall as the hype fades.

3. **Ignoring stop-losses**

Failing to use stop-loss orders means riding coins all the way down. One beginner watched their altcoin dip from $5 to $1 without protection, losing nearly their whole investment.

4. **Risking the entire portfolio**

Going "all in" leaves no room for error. One big drop wipes out everything, while small, careful bets let you live to try again.

5. **Forgetting security practices**

Using weak passwords or leaving coins on exchanges puts investments at risk of hacks or scams. One investor found their balance gone overnight after leaving funds on a shady platform.

6. **Ignoring transaction fees**

High fees on trades and transfers eat into profits, shrinking gains and turning a winning trade into a losing one.

7. **Falling for herd mentality**

Following the crowd into "the next big thing" can backfire. Many rushed into Dogecoin at its peak then panicked as prices crashed, following the next herd elsewhere.

8. **Overleveraging**

Trading with borrowed funds when new to crypto can multiply losses quickly. Some see liquidations erase their capital in a flash.

9. **Neglecting to take profits**

Holding forever in hopes of higher gains, some investors watch strong positions fade back to their entry point or worse.

10. **Trusting scams and quick-rich schemes**

Scams promising triple returns lure beginners. One example: an investor bought into a "guaranteed 10x" project announced on Telegram, only to lose all their funds when the creators vanished.

Risk Management Strategies

Diversifying across different coins and sectors reduces the risk of a single failure ending your progress. For instance, a balanced portfolio might hold 60 percent in Bitcoin and Ethereum, 20 percent in established altcoins, and 20 percent in cash or stablecoins. Setting clear risk limits helps protect you; never invest more than you are comfortable losing. Position sizing ensures that no single trade can threaten your entire account. Stop-loss orders can automatically limit losses when prices move against you. Every purchase should follow a risk-versus-reward mindset, where you carefully weigh potential losses against possible gains before buying. Sticking to these habits, even on turbulent days, keeps your footing steady. When unexpected events strike, such as flash crashes or hacks, you respond with your plan instead of reacting in panic.

Becoming aware of risk and learning how to manage it puts you ahead of most new investors. Understanding common pitfalls and keeping emotions under control gives you the tools to stay balanced and confident. This mindset helps you think long term and face challenges and scams with clarity. Staying alert and practicing consistent caution allows you to protect what you build while continuing to explore new opportunities.

Identifying Scams and Building Investor Resilience

After experiencing the sharp ups and downs of crypto prices, every investor feels their emotions pulling them in risky directions. Markets rise and fall in dramatic swings, tempting many to act on excitement, fear, or blind hope that luck alone will protect their money. The truth is that volatile conditions are exactly what scammers and fraudsters rely on. When emotions run high, it becomes harder to pause, think clearly, and spot warning signs before sending funds or acting on suspicious opportunities. That's when costly mistakes happen.

Criminals use increasingly clever tactics to exploit investor trust. Phishing scams, for example, involve fake websites or emails designed to trick you into revealing your login details or private keys. These often look almost identical to legitimate crypto sites or exchanges. Rug pulls occur when a project team launches a new cryptocurrency or decentralized finance token, builds excitement, collects investor funds, and then disappears, leaving behind worthless coins. Ponzi schemes lure people with promises of high, steady returns but pay early investors with money from new ones. Once the flow of fresh cash stops, the scheme collapses, and most participants lose everything. Fake giveaways are another common trap on social media, where accounts claim they can double your coins if you send some first, but nothing ever comes back.

Spotting these tricks starts with paying attention to details. Be wary of vague or missing information about who is behind a coin or platform. Anonymous teams often avoid accountability. Promises of guaranteed profits or fast riches break the basic rules of real investing. If it sounds too good to be true, it almost always is. Sudden social media hype with little substance, especially when many influencers promote the same project at once, is another major warning sign. Projects without clear whitepapers, working products, or open community discussions are red flags. Legitimate ventures usually share open-source code and undergo independent audits to prove transparency, while scams often skip these entirely.

To check whether a project is genuine, start by reading its whitepaper carefully. Look for clear explanations, achievable goals, and a realistic timeline. Research the team's background using professional profiles or past work in blockchain development. Community discussions on Reddit or established crypto forums can reveal important concerns that official channels may hide. A few hours of due diligence can save you from losses that take months or even years to recover. Check if the project or its smart contracts have been reviewed by recognized security auditors. Before putting any money in, see if news about the project comes from trusted sources, not just anonymous Twitter threads or Telegram groups.

Keeping your crypto safe day to day requires a few consistent habits. Always use established exchanges and wallets with a proven reputation. Double-check website URLs before logging in, since phishing attacks often use addresses that look almost identical to real ones but differ by a single letter. Enable two-factor authentication on every account to make hacking far more difficult. Never share your private key, seed phrase, or wallet backup with anyone, no matter what they promise or offer.

Cases like the Squid Game token rug pull show exactly what can go wrong. The token's creators rode a wave of hype, built a website and a Twitter presence, then vanished with millions after the price spiked, leaving buyers with nothing. A bit of deeper research would have quickly shown that none of the original show's creators or

Netflix had any involvement or approval. No audit, no transparent team, and no verified partnership were all clear signs to walk away.

Short-term thinking often fuels the success of scammers. Chasing viral coins or quick returns might look smart at first, but it usually ends in sudden crashes or scams that erase profits overnight. Real stories repeat the same lesson. One trader jumped into ten meme coins during a bull run and briefly saw massive paper profits, only to lose nearly everything when nine of them collapsed. Meanwhile, investors who focused on solid projects, practiced dollar-cost averaging, held diversified portfolios, and avoided hype grew their wealth gradually but consistently over time.

Steady investing is safer and builds both confidence and resilience. Mistakes are part of every investor's path. The most successful crypto investors are not the ones who never lose, but the ones who learn, adapt, and recover smarter after setbacks. Keep a record of every investment, including the reason behind each decision, and revisit your goals regularly. Reacting emotionally to every price movement leads to regret, but responding with patience and a plan pays off. Engage with other thoughtful investors, share experiences, and learn from both your wins and your missteps.

Staying vigilant protects your assets, but each choice builds trust in your own process. Keep learning, refining your approach, and surrounding yourself with reliable information and level-headed voices. This is how lasting confidence grows and how you stay one step ahead of the next wave of market hype and deception.

Now that you understand the risks and common pitfalls in crypto investing, you can approach the market with a clear plan and steady mindset. By managing volatility through smart strategies like diversification, risk limits, and stop-losses, you protect your investments from sudden shocks and emotional decisions. Staying vigilant against scams and hype means you keep your hard-earned money safe and focused on legitimate opportunities. With these tools in hand, you're ready to build a balanced portfolio that aligns with your goals, navigate unpredictable markets confidently, and grow your crypto wealth over time.

CHAPTER 22

CRYPTO TAXES AND LEGAL CONSIDERATIONS

Have you ever paused mid-transaction, wondering how the government views that trade or sale of your cryptocurrency? Or perhaps you've asked yourself if it matters to keep a record every time you swap one token for another, even when the amounts seem small. If these questions have crossed your mind, you're not alone. The world of crypto taxes and legal rules can feel like a maze, where every move might trigger hidden obligations and unexpected paperwork.

This chapter steps into that complex landscape, bringing clarity to what really counts, why recordkeeping matters, and how staying organized keeps you in control. Understanding the full picture is not only about following the rules but also about protecting yourself and your profits. Knowing how to manage taxes and legal responsibilities turns confusion into confidence, helping you navigate your crypto journey with precision and peace of mind, no matter your experience level.

Understanding Crypto Taxation and Tracking Transactions

Understanding How Countries Tax Crypto

People across the world ask the same question: How does my government tax cryptocurrency? No matter where you live, the answer almost always starts the same way. Most countries, including the United States, the European Union, the United Kingdom, Canada, and Australia, treat cryptocurrencies as property or assets rather than actual money. This distinction has major consequences for how trading, storing, and spending are taxed.

In the United States, every time you sell crypto, trade it for another coin, or use it to buy goods or services, you trigger what's called a taxable event. The IRS requires you to pay capital gains tax on any profit you earn. If you mine, stake, or otherwise earn cryptocurrency, that counts as income and comes with its own set of rules. Simply buying and holding coins without selling does not create any tax obligation until you eventually sell or exchange them.

Things aren't much different in the European Union or United Kingdom. There, selling, swapping, earning, and spending crypto are all reportable. Canada follows a similar approach: the sale, trade, or even conversion between coins is a taxable event. Australia taxes most crypto activity through capital gains tax, so even exchanging one token for another is something the authorities want to know about.

Readers often wonder: Will the government notice a small purchase or casual trade? The fact is, even trades between tokens, or spending your coins on something small, should be tracked. A scenario might help: You buy Bitcoin, then use some to purchase a cup of coffee, and a week later send some to a friend in another country. Each activity might trigger income or capital gains tax, depending on the jurisdiction. From a tax perspective, every time crypto changes hands, so does your tax obligation.

What Makes Crypto Tracking Tricky

Investing in traditional stocks or real estate is usually straightforward. You buy shares in a brokerage account, collect dividends, and sell later. Everything stays in one account with clean records. Crypto doesn't work that way.

The speed and variety of crypto transactions mean a single investor might juggle dozens or even hundreds of trades per year. Prices change minute to minute, so the "cost basis" - the price you paid for something that determines your gains or losses - is constantly shifting. When you add transfers between exchanges and wallets, it becomes very easy to lose track.

Consider a typical hobbyist trader. They buy Ethereum on one exchange, then transfer it to a private wallet. From there, they might swap part of it for Solana using a decentralized exchange. Later, they purchase a digital artwork (NFT) with some leftover ETH. Each move happens at different prices, times, and fee structures. Every action affects what you owe at tax time, so keeping accurate and organized records is essential to staying compliant.

Steps for Tracking Trades, Gains, and Losses

Good recordkeeping is not optional. Track every crypto move with care, even if the numbers seem small. Here's a structured approach that keeps things organized:

- List transaction dates, from purchases to trades to sales
- Record the exact amount and name of the coin or token
- Capture buy/sell prices at the transaction moment, in your local currency

- Save records of network, trading, or exchange fees, you often get to subtract these from your gains
- Note the type of transaction: was it a buy, sell, trade, stake reward, or gift?
- Maintain documentation, like receipts, transaction IDs, and screenshots when possible

Even minor actions, like sending coins to a new wallet or swapping a small amount, add up over a year. Missing even a single transaction can snowball into trouble during an audit. Accuracy is the best defense.

Software That Makes Life Easier

Manual record-keeping quickly becomes overwhelming. Crypto tax software tools like CoinTracker, Koinly, and TaxBit can help. These services connect directly to most popular exchanges and wallets.

- Import all your transaction data instantly from your exchange accounts
- Sync wallet transactions, including deposits and withdrawals
- Review auto-generated tax reports, including calculations for gains, losses, and cost basis
- Find flagged issues, like missing or duplicated transactions

Always check the automatic reports for errors or missing information before filing. The more sources you have, the more likely you'll spot duplicate records or overlooked fees.

An Example That Covers Every Scenario

Consider a reader who buys $1,000 worth of Bitcoin on Coinbase. Step one: record the date, amount, and fees. They transfer $500 in BTC to a private wallet. This action is not taxable, but it still needs to be tracked for accurate recordkeeping. Next, they trade $300 worth of BTC for Ethereum on a decentralized exchange. That trade is a taxable event, so they should note the value on the trading day and the price of the ETH received. Finally, they sell the ETH on another exchange for dollars. That sale is also a taxable event, and all details should be logged. Each swap or sale requires updating your records with the latest figures.

Staying organized and informed keeps your investments safe and compliant, building a strong habit that will serve you well throughout your crypto journey.

Compliance, Audit Preparation, and Record-Keeping Best Practices

As you actively track every gain, loss, and transaction in your crypto portfolio, there's another level of safety you need for full protection: preparation for an audit or sudden regulatory review. Just as tax frameworks and tracking tools give structure to your trading history, audit readiness goes a step further by demanding meticulous records and clear explanations for every movement of funds. Audits can be triggered by a range of scenarios, anything from a misreported decimal point to discrepancies between your filings and records collected by exchanges or third parties to completely random selection. Tax authorities are increasingly matching wallet activity and exchange data against declared income. They can request access to every transaction that might shift your balance, including incoming transfers, outgoing payments, staking rewards, and even seemingly minor conversions between stablecoins.

It helps to stay ready with an audit file for each year. You should be prepared to provide information such as

- Complete lists of wallet and exchange addresses you control (both hot and cold storage)
- Detailed transaction logs from exchanges and wallets (CSV or spreadsheet format)

- Screenshots or PDF statements showing trade histories and balances
- Records of wallet-to-wallet transfers, including explanations for each transfer
- Supporting documentation for staking, lending, or DeFi activities
- A log of fiat on-ramps or off-ramps, showing bank deposits or withdrawals connected to crypto transactions

Regularly updating this file means you won't scramble to track down fragments of information years later. If an auditor requests clarification, you can quickly supply any document or screenshot to prove your case. Imagine facing an inquiry about a major swap made three years prior. If all it takes is opening your digital folder, finding the transaction hash, attached explanation, and a PDF from the relevant exchange, you save time and reduce stress. Missing or incomplete records only increase audit duration and the risk of penalties.

Rules around crypto taxation evolve as governments adapt to new forms of trading and investment. Each year might bring changes: mandatory reporting of wallet holdings, stricter reporting on offshore exchanges, or requirements to declare NFT transactions. Ignoring these shifts puts your compliance at risk. Subscribing to reliable sources keeps you ahead. Watch for updates published by national tax authorities, such as the IRS, HMRC, or the ATO, or alerts from reputable tax platforms and certified advisors. Consider setting a calendar reminder for a yearly portfolio review so you routinely double-check for changes affecting crypto reporting.

Keeping up with these changes means using tools that incorporate new requirements. Many leading tax software providers update their systems after every policy shift, allowing you to adapt quickly. But never assume automation covers every detail. Manual checklists help. Review the following annually:

- Are all exchanges and wallets accounted for?
- Have new asset types (like NFTs or DeFi tokens) been included in records?
- Are all deposit and withdrawal records accessible and backed up?
- Is each transaction annotated with its business purpose and context?
- Has the software or template you use incorporated recent legal changes?

Maintaining pristine records starts with a simple, workable system. Begin with a master spreadsheet listing every transaction by date, type, asset, amount, source, and destination. For added security, download and store all monthly account statements from every exchange or wallet. These should be saved in both a secure cloud folder and an offline storage device, ideally with encrypted backups. Alongside your automated tracking, keep a folder of "manual notes", text files, or PDFs describing the reason for transfers, staking arrangements, or asset swaps.

Annotating transactions clarifies intent. If you move ETH from Exchange A to a private wallet, record in your log, "Transfer for cold storage, no sale occurred." For a staking reward, attach a brief note describing the protocol and the approximate APY at the time. This habit eliminates guesswork during future tax returns or audits. Spreadsheets act as a safety net if automated tools miss or misclassify a transaction.

Practically, thorough record-keeping transforms tax preparation. Investors who keep annotated records, digital receipts, and backup logs can generate annual tax reports within hours instead of days. In several cases, an investor faced with an audit provided a zip file containing all documents, transaction hashes, and explanations enabling a short, low-stress audit rather than a protracted investigation.

Compliance brings more than audit survival. Only rock-solid records protect against suspicion and fines as regulations change and authorities use blockchain analytics to trace funds across networks. Though crypto might appear anonymous, that's a fading myth, wallet addresses are now mapped, and exchanges report activity as standard practice. Confidence comes from knowing you can answer any question about your portfolio, no matter who's asking.

This peace of mind lets you focus on long-term growth, knowing that your foundation is solid. You'll face law changes, or that unwelcome letter from the tax authority, not with panic, but with the certainty that your preparation puts you firmly in control of your financial future.

Now that you understand how cryptocurrency is taxed and why careful tracking and record-keeping are essential, you're equipped to navigate this complex landscape with confidence. By staying organized, using the right tools, and keeping up with changing rules, you can protect yourself from costly mistakes and audits while maximizing your investment potential. This solid foundation allows you to focus on growing your crypto portfolio strategically and legally, turning your ambitions into real financial progress without the stress of uncertainty.

CHAPTER 23
THE FUTURE OF CRYPTO – WEB3, AI, AND BEYOND

"Why should I trust a computer program with my money when banks have always handled it?" That question echoes in the minds of many who hear about crypto and blockchain for the first time. It's a fair concern; after all, handing over control to technology rather than familiar institutions feels risky and confusing. But what if that very shift could unlock new opportunities for managing your finances, proving your identity, or even owning pieces of things you never thought possible? As technologies like blockchain and artificial intelligence evolve, they're quietly reshaping how we interact with money and information. These aren't just abstract ideas for experts; they're tools that anyone eager to learn can use to take more control over their financial future. Understanding the true value behind each innovation without succumbing to hype is crucial for navigating this new landscape. This chapter invites you to step beyond skepticism and explore how these emerging technologies might fit into your journey toward smarter investing and greater financial freedom.

Technological Shifts: Blockchain, AI, and Emerging Trends

Few changes promise as much for personal finance and opportunity as blockchain. At its core, blockchain is a record-keeping system that works without a central authority, letting users interact, earn, lend, and invest on new terms. The shift to decentralized finance, or DeFi, is already unlocking possibilities that mainstream banks can't match. Imagine lending money on a platform that connects you directly with borrowers without needing a bank's approval. These peer-to-peer platforms let people set their own rates, sometimes in countries where opening a bank account is hard or where traditional loans cost too much to make sense. Sending money home from abroad follows similar rules. Blockchains allow remittances across borders for a tiny fraction of what money-transfer services charge. For millions of families, that small difference in cost means more money where it's needed.

Beyond moving cash, blockchain is also changing the way we prove and manage who we are. Right now, personal details like driver's licenses, school records, work credentials, sit in government or company silos. If you lose a password or paperwork, that can mean headaches or lost chances. A digital identity built on blockchain puts individuals in control instead. Credentials live in a crypto wallet you manage, protected by encryption. For example, think about a freelancer wanting to show proof of skills to a potential client. Using a blockchain-based resume, they can securely share only the pieces needed, with no central authority in the way. This approach makes moving between jobs, countries, or online platforms safer and faster.

Ownership, too, looks different on blockchains. Tokenization turns assets into digital tokens that represent real-world value, opening up ownership to a wider pool of investors. Small investors can now own fractions instead of needing thousands to buy a slice of a start-up or a chunk of real estate. Non-fungible tokens, or NFTs, draw the most buzz. Digital art is just the start. Items like rare collectibles, event tickets, or shares in a classic car can all be managed and traded on-chain. These changes aren't just for tech enthusiasts; they give everyone a shot at new types of value.

Crypto's next promise is merging with artificial intelligence. One way this happens is with AI-powered trading bots. Normally, managing a set of crypto investments takes time and skill. Some projects let users tap into pre-built bots that analyze market data, automate trades, and even shift strategies on their own. In another trend, blockchains are being used to verify where the data that feeds AI models comes from. Since AI models rely on giant sets of information, trust is everything. A blockchain trail makes it easier to spot tampering and protect against misinformation, which is helpful for things like medical research or legal analysis.

That said, not every new combo of crypto and AI works out as promised. Some companies claim "intelligent blockchains" that make decisions on their own, but in reality, these systems often struggle outside controlled settings. A well-known project in 2023 offered AI-based security on the blockchain, boasting instant scam detection. Early users found that, while some fraud was caught, the system missed subtler tricks and had trouble adapting to new threats. While AI tools in crypto can automate tasks and reduce manual labor, human oversight is still necessary. A trading algorithm might boost profit on good days but crash in a volatile market. Investors who trust these systems without understanding the risks sometimes end up disappointed.

Maintaining composure and a steady checklist is crucial when navigating the constantly changing crypto world. The strongest projects rest on sound code, regular audits, and open communities. Useful crypto products solve real problems like lowering transfer costs or helping manage identity. Look for signs of real adoption: are people using the platform, and do experienced developers back it up? Regulatory trends matter as well. If a project dodges questions about compliance, that's a warning sign.

Red flags stand out with a little practice. Vague whitepapers that dodge technical details, big promises backed only by a famous face, or tokens with no clear use case often signal more hype than value. A solid investment asks for careful thought, not just excitement.

Curiosity leads the way, but mixing skepticism with excitement helps avoid costly mistakes. As the ground shifts under your feet, staying open while vetting each chance on its facts, not just feelings, offers the best shot for safe progress. Every new feature or product can hint at where the future is heading, and the sharpest paths combine learning, patience, and self-protection as these opportunities take shape.

Practical Implications: Your Role, Opportunities, and Sensible Strategies

As crypto and AI merge further into daily life, they create tools and opportunities for everyone, not just early tech adopters. Blockchains automate and record financial and legal activities. AI sorts data, finds patterns, and helps people make decisions. Combining these forces means regular people will soon handle their money, work, and digital identity in new ways. For investors, freelancers, or employees, learning to use these tools will be as basic as learning to use a smartphone is today.

Picture yourself investing using decentralized finance (DeFi) platforms instead of a traditional bank. You might deposit coins into a decentralized savings protocol that pays higher interest for holding your assets. Unlike a regular bank account, your funds are spread across a smart contract code that runs itself based on set rules making transactions fast and transparent. When you need a loan or want to trade, you interact directly with the platform, skipping paperwork and extra fees. No need to trust a single company; instead, you trust the code and the network.

For creatives, non-fungible tokens (NFTs) give a path to new income. An author, musician, or designer can release a limited-edition digital product as an NFT. Each token proves authenticity and ownership, so fans can resell or trade digital collectibles the same way rare comic books or vinyl records once were. A small royalty fee goes back to the creator each time an NFT changes hands, making creative work more profitable and sustainable. This same technology may extend to intellectual property like patents for inventors or thesis papers for scholars giving anyone an easy and trackable way to license or share their work.

Small business owners and freelancers could join decentralized autonomous organizations (DAOs). These groups, run fully by code and community votes, pool resources for business ventures, investments, or passion projects. As a member, you might help vote on where funds go or submit your ideas for the group to back. The process is open, and all decisions are stored on a blockchain for everyone to see. As more companies experiment with DAOs, professionals will need to understand these governance models and the digital wallets used to participate.

Another change comes in the form of blockchain-verified identity. Instead of relying on a stack of paper documents or passwords, you hold a digital credential in your crypto wallet, a record that only you control, proving your skills, work history, or education. Employers or clients can instantly check these badges, speeding up hiring, making remote work easier, and letting gig workers collect references from anywhere in the world. This shifts the traditional resume and job-seeking process to a globally trusted, secure, and instantly accessible format.

Stepping back, the question becomes: how do you spot the next opportunity without taking on too much risk? Success in crypto rarely comes from chasing every trend. Instead, set clear rules to evaluate what is worth your time and money. Here's a simple framework:

1. **Real-world use:** Does the project solve a real problem or make something easier for people or businesses?
2. **Team transparency:** Who is building the project? Can you find their names, past work, and public commitments?

3. **Technology credibility:** Has the technology been tested? Are there audits, code reviews, or partnerships with reliable companies?
4. **Community support:** Is there active discussion on forums, social media, or developer chats? Do real users contribute and point out flaws or suggest improvements?
5. **Roadmap and whitepaper:** Does the project have a clear plan? Can you understand what they want to build and why?

Before investing, read the whitepaper closely. Look for clear writing, honest discussion of risks, and simple diagrams of how the system works. Caution if you notice grand promises but no details. Check the leadership; can you verify their past success? Search for recent updates and if promises are being met. For example, many early investors in Ethereum saw progress on long-term milestones and engagement from a skilled team. By contrast, meme coins, or short-lived hype tokens, often lacked serious documentation, leadership, or genuine community support, and many disappeared as fast as they grew.

To stay ahead but avoid hype fatigue, create a personal strategy. Only track two or three projects and document why you chose them and your exit or review plan. Split your portfolio with strict rules, capping how much you risk on any one idea. Write down your reasons for every decision and revisit them monthly, not daily. Reliable success builds on patience, skepticism, and a willingness to learn as the tech changes.

Make ongoing learning a habit. Follow developer blogs from trusted people. Listen to select podcasts known for balanced insight, not hype. Join one or two online groups where people challenge bad ideas and engage in open discussion. If you want to go further, look for short, focused courses on concepts you don't understand yet.

Most of all, remember that adapting to the crypto future is about steady effort, not wild bets. Be curious, but demand evidence before acting. Grow your skills reading contract code, understanding wallet basics, and using simple DeFi tools so you're prepared to judge each new wave of change as it arrives. Holding onto these habits gives you the best chance to benefit, no matter where crypto and AI lead next.

Now that we understand how blockchain and AI are reshaping finance, identity, and ownership, the path forward is clear: success comes from blending curiosity with careful judgment. These technologies open doors to new ways of investing, working, and creating value if you approach them with patience, learn steadily, and rely on real evidence over hype. By focusing on projects that solve genuine problems, backed by transparent teams and active communities, you position yourself to navigate this evolving landscape wisely. With a solid strategy and ongoing education, you can turn emerging crypto opportunities into lasting financial growth, making smart choices today that build your wealth tomorrow.

CHAPTER 24
YOUR ACTION PLAN – FROM BEGINNER TO INVESTOR

Nearly half of all new investors quit within their first year, not because they lack funds but because they struggle to turn plans into action. It's easy to get stuck reading about strategies or waiting for the perfect moment to start. Yet investing isn't a spectator sport; it requires setting clear goals, making choices, and learning through experience.

Taking that first step can feel daunting, as uncertainty, risk, and complex language create barriers that keep many people on the sidelines. But confidence doesn't come from theory alone; it grows through doing. This chapter focuses on crossing that line from hesitation to hands-on investing, helping beginners build a foundation rooted in purpose and clarity. By taking practical actions such as defining what you want, choosing investments that match your comfort level, and tracking your progress, you begin to shape your own story as an investor, one decision at a time.

Laying the Groundwork: Planning Your First Steps in Investing

Setting clear and realistic investing goals shapes every decision you make next. Picture what success means for you. Some want to build long-term wealth to beat inflation. Others hope to earn extra monthly income. Begin with a personal statement written for your eyes only honest and specific. Try something like, "I want to see my initial $1,000 grow over three years so I can plan a future trip," or "I want to learn how to generate income through staking rewards and see my crypto savings grow by 6% each year." A clear reason builds focus, and that focus keeps you on track when markets are noisy.

Personal finance always comes with risk. Crypto investing involves more ups and downs than a savings account, so it's important to think seriously about your comfort with risk. Take a minute to jot down some honest answers:

- Are you okay seeing the value of your investments change by 10–20% or more in a short time?
- How would you feel if you logged in and saw your portfolio drop in value for a few weeks in a row?
- Are these funds set aside for long-term goals, or would you need them soon for emergencies?
- Will losing your investment make you lose sleep—or can you treat it as a lesson?

Matching your investing goals and comfort with risk lays the foundation for every smart decision that follows. If dramatic price swings make you anxious, focus on a slow and steady path toward growth. If you are more comfortable with uncertainty, you can take on a little more risk, but always within clear limits.

Once you understand your motivation, turn your attention to selecting your first cryptocurrencies and a reliable platform. For most beginners, ease of use, security, and access to major coins matter most. Bitcoin and Ethereum are excellent starting points. Both have stood the test of time, with large global communities and proven stability. If you want variety, consider adding a third coin such as Solana or Cardano, but stay away from tokens that promise instant wealth or appear only because of online trends.

Next, choose a trustworthy exchange. A crypto exchange is a platform where you can buy, sell, or trade digital currencies. Look for one that offers a simple sign-up process and strong security. Well-known choices for new investors include Coinbase, Kraken, and Binance US. Before you register, review their password protection policies, confirm that they support two-factor authentication, and compare fees. High transaction costs can quietly eat into your gains. Avoid smaller or lesser-known exchanges, especially those with flashy marketing, unclear information, or reports of frozen withdrawals.

Finally, consider how you will store your crypto. Some exchanges hold coins on your behalf, which is convenient at first, but storing them in your own wallet gives you more control and long-term security. For beginners, using the exchange's built-in wallet is fine. As you gain confidence, learn how to transfer your assets to a private app called a non-custodial wallet. Choose one with an easy recovery process, strong reviews, and reliable customer support.

Building your starter portfolio means choosing just two or three coins and spreading your money between them. Here's an example for someone investing $1,000:

- $600 in Bitcoin (BTC)
- $300 in Ethereum (ETH)
- $100 in Solana (SOL) or Cardano (ADA)

Start small, only invest what you're willing to lose, and treat every dollar as a tool for learning. Avoid over-diversifying; too many coins make tracking and research a headache. A focused approach gives you a front-row seat to the basics, from price moves to real-world news affecting your holdings.

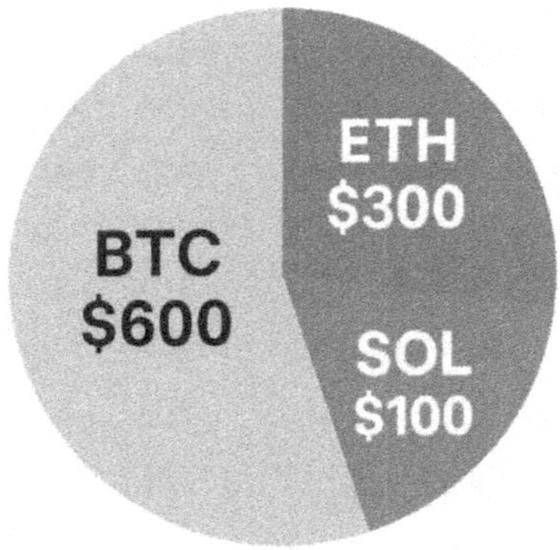

Now you need a tracking system. The habit of recording buys, sells, and balances keeps you engaged and prevents emotional reactions. For many, a simple spreadsheet works best. Columns for date, coin, amount, price paid, and current value show clearly what you own. Some prefer a free tracker app made for crypto, which often links directly to exchanges and updates in real time. Or use a notebook; consistency matters more than the tool. On payday or at a set point each month, review and add notes on any important events or price swings. A log helps you make sense of the journey and adds clarity every time you check in.

Getting started with goal setting, coin selection, and tracking habits puts you in control. Every recorded decision builds confidence, turning theory into clear action. This foundation gives you the experience to move forward, and your first portfolio becomes more than a collection of coins; it's your training ground, ready to teach you with every step you take. The next section guides you through growing this starter approach into real-world learning, so you build up both skills and wealth as you go.

Taking Action: Building Confidence Through Practical Experience

Every successful crypto investor remembers their first steps: the nerves, the uncertainty, maybe even a bit of excitement as they placed a tiny buy order or explored a new wallet. That sense of moving from theory to practice unlocks real growth. Having set your broad goals and carefully built your first portfolio, you now get to build on your courage and organization by learning directly through hands-on action. The most valuable teacher in the crypto world is experience; each mini-experiment builds confidence in ways that planning alone can't. Even small steps are solid progress, letting you see for yourself how markets, platforms, and currencies behave in real time.

Imagine someone buying $50 worth of Ethereum for the very first time. They choose a well-known, widely supported coin, compare a few apps to find one that feels straightforward, and set up a secure wallet before pressing "Buy." Almost immediately, they notice that confirmation times vary and that transaction fees can reduce the total. A few minutes later, seeing ETH appear in their wallet feels like crossing a threshold from spectator to genuine investor. They jot down notes about what went smoothly, what was confusing, and what surprised them. That first trade becomes the foundation for the next step: maybe researching why fees change throughout the day or testing another exchange with a small amount. Bit by bit, these small actions build understanding that lasts.

Active investing does not require large sums of money or advanced technical knowledge. Most beginners find that confidence grows each time they take a manageable risk and review the outcome with curiosity and patience. For example, someone might set aside $25 worth of a token to experiment with staking, not to chase high rewards but to learn how platforms pay earnings and process withdrawals. By checking their staking dashboard weekly, tracking rewards, and noting any issues or delays, they gain insights that reading alone could never provide.

You can turn these small experiments into steady habits with a few simple tools. A compact notebook, digital or paper, works perfectly as an investing journal. After each trade or new experience, take a moment to answer a few short prompts that help you reflect on what you learned, what worked, and what to adjust next:

- What worked that I might use again?
- What was more complicated than I expected?
- What new question do I have after seeing the results?
- What would I try next time to improve the result?

Spread these reflections out in bullet points or a quick table if that feels easier. The trick is to capture your own thinking while the memory is fresh, making it easy to spot patterns and build reliable routines over time. Spreadsheets help too: track the dates of trades, platforms used, fees paid, and changes in portfolio size. You'll soon see that every entry is a clue for better decisions down the road.

To keep decisions steady and avoid being rattled by impulsive news alerts, try using a "pause and verify" checklist before each move. Have you double-checked wallet addresses? Have you skimmed recent news or social media about the project? Are fees within your expected range? If anything feels off or confusing, stop and review. This quick, repeatable habit turns what used to be scary into a straightforward part of your investing plan.

Here's how you can put learning-by-doing into practice:

First, recognize that small, live experiments teach you what books and videos can't. Handling even a modest trade lets you feel how platforms work, see real numbers change, and get the emotional experience of gaining, or losing, a dollar or two in value. These lessons last because you lived them, not just studied them.

Try this step-by-step activity:

1. Pick a well-known coin such as BTC or ETH.

2. Buy a small amount (as little as $10 if the app allows it).

3. Record in your tracker or notebook everything you notice about the process; timing, fees, ease of use.

4. Watch how your portfolio number moves for a few days.

5. Answer reflection questions:

- How did the transaction compare to what I expected?
- What did I learn from seeing real price changes?
- Would I do anything differently on my next trade?

6. Challenge yourself to repeat with a new coin, a different exchange, or a feature like staking or swapping, recording each new insight.

Throughout this book, you will keep building on these action-based skills. Each new topic and strategy connects to practical investing steps, allowing your experience to grow alongside your portfolio and knowledge. Testing ideas, reflecting honestly, and recording what you learn takes fear out of the process and helps you create your own guide for staying safe, adapting to changing markets, and developing as an investor. Every action, whether successful or not, lays the groundwork for smarter decisions and stronger confidence each time you step into the crypto world.

Now that you have built a solid foundation by setting clear goals, choosing your first coins, and establishing habits to track and reflect on your progress, you are ready to move forward with confidence from planning into active learning through real-world experience. Each small trade and every note you take sharpens your understanding and builds resilience against the ups and downs of crypto markets. By embracing this hands-on approach, you turn theory into practical knowledge that grows alongside your portfolio. As you continue on this journey, these early steps will prepare you to explore new strategies, manage risks wisely, and steadily build the skills and confidence needed to make your crypto investments work for your financial future.

BE THE VOICE THAT INSPIRES FINANCIAL FREEDOM

One of life's greatest truths is that when we share what we have learned, we empower others to grow. Every insight we pass on can light the way for someone just beginning their journey.

Think for a moment about how you felt when you first considered investing in cryptocurrency. Were you excited by the possibilities? Are you uncertain about the risks involved? Are you curious but hesitant to take the first step?

Now picture another reader standing in that same place. They are hearing about Bitcoin, Ethereum, altcoins, NFTs, and blockchain, but they are not sure where to start or how to invest wisely without losing confidence.

This is where your review can make a real difference. By sharing your honest reflections, you help others decide whether this guide offers the strategies, clarity, and encouragement they need to move forward.

Your words can inspire confidence and remind others that financial freedom begins with knowledge, discipline, and courage. Thank you for being part of this journey. Your voice matters, and by leaving a review, you are helping make cryptocurrency investing more accessible for every reader who follows in your footsteps.

CONCLUSION

As you reach this final page, take a moment to reflect on how far you have come. If you began this journey uncertain about crypto, unsure of what it really is or how everyday people actually profit from it, you are not alone. Crypto investing can seem mysterious and intimidating, full of technical jargon, wild price swings, and headlines that make it sound either like a perfect get-rich-quick scheme or an elaborate scam. But now you hold something most newcomers never achieve: a clear understanding of what the world of digital assets truly offers, and practical strategies for building lasting wealth.

You have learned that success in crypto does not require genius-level tech skills. It requires curiosity, common sense, a solid plan, and the commitment to treat your financial future as something worth learning for. Throughout these pages, you have discovered that crypto's potential for wealth-building is not reserved for computer scientists or Silicon Valley insiders. It belongs to anyone who prepares, studies, and approaches investing with discipline and patience.

Crypto rewards those who are ready and patient. One of the biggest mistakes new investors make is believing they must act quickly—

jumping on trends, chasing the hottest coins, or trying to time the market. You now know the truth: the investors who succeed, whether by holding strong assets like Bitcoin and Ethereum or by exploring new opportunities such as NFTs and DeFi, are the ones who do their homework first. They research before investing, create a clear risk management plan, and balance their portfolios based on long-term goals rather than online noise.

Let's face it, there will always be hype in crypto. There will always be people promising quick riches or the next big "moonshot." But as you have seen, there are smarter ways to build and sustain real wealth. You do not need to abandon common sense or rush in blindly. Your power lies in your ability to understand the rules, recognize opportunities, and stay calm when others lose control. You already hold one of the greatest advantages in this space: you know you do not know everything, and you are willing to keep learning.

That humility and curiosity set you apart. Too many investors believe they must predict every move or understand blockchain technology in full detail. The truth is simpler: you only need a thoughtful plan that fits your personal financial goals and comfort with risk. Whether your aim is long-term growth, passive income, or diversification beyond traditional assets, your journey begins with a few key steps that anyone can take. No coding skills or full-time trading are required.

So what comes next? The answer is simple: action. Over the next 90 days, you have a real opportunity to take control, move forward, and start building your own foundation for digital wealth.

Here are practical steps to put what you have learned into motion:

Review your finances honestly. Decide what portion of your income or savings you can safely allocate to crypto. Remember, starting small is not just a saying; it is how nearly every successful investor begins. Even a modest investment allows you to gain experience without risking more than you can afford to lose.

Secure your accounts. Open accounts only with reputable exchanges and wallets. Turn on two-factor authentication, back up your private keys, and double-check where sensitive information is stored. In crypto, protecting your capital is not only wise but essential.

Choose your first assets carefully. Apply what you have learned about the different types of cryptocurrencies, from established coins like Bitcoin and Ethereum to promising altcoins or tokens with genuine utility. Ask yourself: What problem does this project solve? Who is behind it? What makes it stand out? The best investments rarely come from hype; they come from understanding and insight.

Build your portfolio slowly, keeping diversity and balance in mind. Allocate your funds across different categories such as blue-chip coins, promising smaller projects, and perhaps a small portion in innovative areas like NFTs or DeFi if you feel ready. Rebalance your portfolio periodically, just as you would with traditional investments.

Keep managing your risks. Set stop-loss orders if you trade, and never invest money you will need in the short term. Use dollar-cost averaging instead of trying to time every high and low. Above all, separate your emotions from daily price movements. The market will swing wildly, but your goal is to stay consistent with your plan.

Explore multiple income strategies at your own pace. You may want to try staking, lending, or earning passive yield through decentralized finance platforms. Start small and research thoroughly before committing. Each tool carries its own risks but also offers the potential for strong returns when used wisely.

Continue your education. The blockchain world evolves quickly, so staying informed is essential. Choose trusted sources such as newsletters, podcasts, and YouTube channels that focus on solid analysis rather than hype. Make a habit of learning something new each week. Over time, these efforts will compound your knowledge just as your investments compound your wealth.

By taking these steps, you will discover something important: building digital wealth is not about luck or perfect timing. It is about process, patience, and the courage to begin even when you do not have every answer. Think of the examples you read earlier in this book. Real investors started with only a few dollars and many questions, made mistakes but learned from them, and steadily built their portfolios over time.

You can do the same. You're already ahead of the curve because you've equipped yourself with knowledge, skepticism, and a commitment to continuous improvement. Every successful crypto investor was once a beginner, unsure of what to do next. The difference between those who thrive and those who falter is simple: action grounded in education and self-discipline.

The reality is that digital finance is not going away; it's only becoming a larger part of the global economy. The old boundaries between asset classes are dissolving. Crypto is no longer a fringe experiment; it's quickly moving into the mainstream, reshaping how people save, invest, and think about money itself. By stepping in now, thoughtfully and responsibly, you position yourself at the forefront of this transformation.

Remember, wealth without limits isn't built overnight. But it is available to anyone willing to start, stay smart, and keep learning. Don't let fear or perfectionism keep you on the sidelines. Every great investor was once a newcomer, every expert once asked their first question, and every thriving portfolio started with a single trade.

In closing, your journey toward digital wealth begins not with a leap, but with a single step, a decision to take control of your financial future. Start small, stay curious, remain disciplined, and make learning a regular habit. Crypto investing rewards those who prepare, who wait, and who act, not rashly, but with purpose.

Your new wealth starts here, today. What you do in the next 90 days could lay the groundwork for a lifetime of financial freedom. So, as you close this book, remember: you don't need to be a technical expert to win in this space. You just need a plan, a willingness to take action, and the resilience to keep going.

This is your invitation. The tools, the knowledge, and the strategies are now yours. Step forward, and let your path to wealth without limits begin now.

www.ingramcontent.com/pod-product-compliance
Lightning Source LLC
Chambersburg PA
CBHW050524240926
51846CB00003B/690
* 9 7 8 1 9 7 0 8 3 9 1 7 3 *